HOME RUN KINGS

HOME RUN KINGS

Alan Minsky

MetroBooks

MetroBooks

An Imprint of Friedman/Fairfax Publishers

© 1995, 1996 by Michael Friedman Publishing Group, Inc.

Library of Congress Cataloging-in-Publication Data

Minsky, Alan, date
    Home run kings / Alan Minsky.
      p.   cm.
    Includes bibliographical references (p.) and index.
    ISBN 1-56799-142-4
    1. Home runs (Baseball). 2. Baseball players--United States.
  3. Baseball--United States--Statistics. I. Title.
GV868.4.M56 1995
796.357'092'2--dc20
[B]   94-27731
                                   CIP

Editor: Nathaniel Marunas
Art Director: Jeff Batzli
Designers: Kevin Ullrich and Stan Stanski
Photography Editors: Susan Mettler and Wendy Missan

Color separations by Advance Laser Graphic Arts (International) Ltd.
Printed in China by Leefung-Asco Printers Ltd.

For bulk purchases and special sales, please contact:
Friedman/Fairfax Publishers
Attention: Sales Department
15 West 26th Street
New York, NY 10010
(212) 685-6610 FAX (212) 685-1307

Photography Credits

© **Allsport USA:** Jonathan Daniel: 74 right; Stephen Dunn: 73 top center; Otto Greule: 17 bottom; Bill Hickey: 17 top left; Jed Jacobsohn: 73 bottom; Joe Patronite: 57 right; Rick Stewart: 16, 69 left

AP/Wide World Photos: 2, 10, 12-13, 15 top, 21 top, 26 bottom, 29 both, 30 left, 33, 35 left, 37 bottom, 40–41, 43 top, 45 both, 48 top left, center, and right, 49 top left, center, and right, 52, 53, 55 both, 56 right, 60, 61 both, 62, 63, 64 top, 65 left, 66 both, 67, 68 top, 69 right, 70 both, 71 both

Archive Photos: 22 bottom

The Brearley Collection, Inc.: 6 bottom, 43 bottom

© **George Burke:** 12 center left

© **Focus on Sports:** 15 bottom left, 21 bottom, 37 top, 39, 40 left, 42 left; © Tom Dipace: 73 top left; © Mickey Palmer: 38; © Jerry Wachter: 54

FPG International: 8, 9, 13 center, 19 right, 20, 30 right, 42 top right, 48 bottom, 49 bottom, 50; © Hy Peskin: 12 bottom left, 15 bottom right, 18, 22 top left and right, 23 top left, center, and right, 25, 26 top, 28, 31, 32, 36, 42 bottom right, 51, 68 bottom; © Jack Zehrt: 23 bottom

National Baseball Library and Archive, Cooperstown, N.Y.: 11 both, 12 top left, 13 right, 14, 17 top right, 19 left, 24, 27, 34, 35 right, 44, 46 top, 47, 58, 59

© **Bob Rosato:** 1, 6 top, 72, 73 top right

© **Don Smith:** 74 left

Sportschrome East/West: © Jeff Carlick: 7, 56 left; Rob Tringali Jr.: 57 left, 75

© **Dave Stock:** 46 bottom

UPI/Bettmann: 64 bottom, 65 right

Dedication

To My Father

Acknowledgments

Special thanks to Nathaniel Marunas,
my parents, my roommates, and the
guys at the Baseball Hall of Fame
library for their assistance and support.

Contents

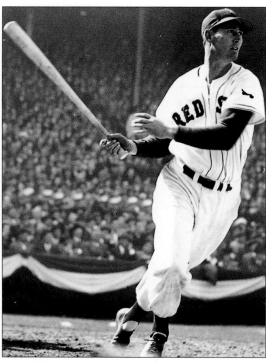

A list of baseball's greatest home run hitters reads like a register of American legends: Babe Ruth, Willie Mays, Henry Aaron, Mickey Mantle, Ted Williams, Joe DiMaggio. No sport has meant as much to the United States as baseball, and no players have captured the imagination of the public quite like its sluggers: Jimmie Foxx, Josh Gibson, Roger Maris, Lou Gehrig, Reggie Jackson, Barry Bonds. This book tells the story of these men and their mythic achievements on the fields of our national pastime.

Baseball is a team game in which the central drama is a battle between two individuals: the pitcher and the batter. The pitcher uses all his skills and savvy to try to deceive the batter. The batter wants to reach base safely. He stands ready, knowing he only has an instant to react to the pitch, to interpret the ball's path and use his finely honed swing to send the ball soaring.

The home run is the ultimate offensive weapon, capable of instantly changing the complexion of the contest and exposing the pitcher's vulnerability. Yet it is unwise to step up to the plate intent on homering. A major league hurler will fool any batter who overswings. Even the greatest sluggers must rely on the basic strategy of carefully watching each pitch and attempting to make full contact with the ball. A home run results from the deployment of a well-disciplined swing—the product of years of practice and lightning-quick reflexes—that generates considerable power. In general, home run hitters swing with a slight uppercut and shift more of their weight forward than do singles hitters, who have more level swings and maintain greater balance in order to direct the placement of their hits. However, all great hitters have distinct batting styles.

A contemporary fan who studies Babe Ruth's swing, photographs of Frank "Home Run" Baker at bat, and a videotape of Henry Aaron's record-breaking 715th home run sees not only great athletes displaying their prowess, but also men who were symbols of their age and their nation. The United States' romance with baseball began around the time of the Civil War (1861–1865), and by 1900 the sport was recognized as the "national pastime." Until the late 1960s baseball reigned unchallenged as the United States'

Virtually all sports fans know that Henry Aaron surpassed Babe Ruth's career home run total in 1974 to become the all-time home run king. Few people remember, however, that in his youth, Aaron—pictured above with manager Fred Haney—was an all-around superstar (rivaled only by Willie Mays) who led the Milwaukee Braves to two consecutive pennants and a World Series championship in the late 1950s.

Reggie Jackson, pictured here late in his career playing for the California Angels, was always an intimidating presence at the plate. Reggie once summed up his philosophy on hitting: "I'd rather hit than have sex. To hit is to show strength....When I'm up there, I'm thinking, 'Try everything you want. Rub up the ball. Move fielders around. Throw me hard stuff, soft stuff. Try anything, I'm still going to hit that ball.' God, do I love to hit that little round sum-bitch out of the park and make 'em say 'Wow!'"

the cultural pantheon. The home run had not been a significant part of the game until Babe Ruth revolutionized the sport with his titanic clouts in the early 1920s. The adoring public was in awe of Ruth and the generation of sluggers that followed him; they watched baseballs that were hit farther than they ever dreamt possible. Ruth went from idol to myth and beyond. Fans who flocked to see him play spent the entire game transfixed by his presence. He was the country's greatest hero, and still remains its premier sporting legend. Succeeding generations of power hitters have vied for Ruth's crown and the adoration that goes along with it, and some have succeeded (though there could only ever be one Babe). Following Ruth, the game's greatest sluggers—Mays, Mantle, DiMaggio, and Aaron, to name a few— became larger-than-life American heroes.

Of course, in the days since Ruth, the term "home run" has entered into common parlance. To say that you have "hit a home run" conveys not merely the achievement of your goals, but spectacular success. The image recalls the infrequency of such success, since a home run—a perfectly fluid, mighty swing that makes pure, unbridled contact, sending the ball into orbit—is a rarity. Home runs occurred only 1.78 times per game in 1993 (out of an average of 250 opportunities per game). When they do fly, what sweetness! What an exhibition of coordination and muscle! The crowd goes wild or, perhaps, sits in stunned, respectful silence.

I play in the San Francisco City Softball League, where the home runs are usually of the inside-the-park variety. However, my team's clean up hitter, Mark Barie, is capable of blasts of near-Ruthian proportions. Once, Barie got all of a pitch, and in a flash the ball cleared the thirty-foot left-field chain-link fence (rarely done) and did not fall to earth until it had passed over eight lanes of freeway (perhaps never before done). What a catharsis it is to witness such clean and powerful contact! Suffice to say, everyone on our team becomes an excited spectator whenever Mark steps in the batter's box, much as the entire baseball-watching public does when today's greatest sluggers—such as Barry Bonds, Frank Thomas, and Ken Griffey, Jr.—dig in for a monster swing.

"He's into his wind-up, here's the pitch...'crack' ...there's a long drive to left-center, way back, it's going, going, gone! Home run!"

favorite spectator sport. While the game's rules have remained basically the same since 1901, the style of play has constantly evolved. Baseball, both through how it is played and through the ever-changing cast of men who play it, is a fundamental part of the American experience.

Baseball literature and journalism, along with photographs and films of ballplayers and their fans, provide a unique perspective on American history. When the game was rugged and violent, were its fans? Was the country? Did the influence of gamblers at the ballyard reflect broader corruption in society? Did the boom in home run hitting and the contemporary decline in base stealing dur-

ing the 1920s betray a society that was beginning to value spectacle over the hard-won rewards of finesse? Did the social elite attend many games? Did women attend games? Were the players family men? Were they from the working class? Did they drink? Do drugs? Could they read? Did they speak English? In this land of immigrants, where ancient cultures intertwined as they never had before, blending into the ever-evolving tapestry of American culture, baseball captured the imagination of all the nation's peoples. Baseball was among the United States' first common languages.

Within an increasingly secular United States, baseball's home run kings held a special place in

The Advent and Evolution of the Home Run

Ty Cobb of the Detroit Tigers was baseball's greatest hitter and most potent offensive threat before Babe Ruth. Cobb possessed a lethal combination of blazing speed, tremendous bat control—which allowed him to hit to all fields—and an unrelenting desire to win. However, like his contemporaries, Cobb rarely hit the ball out of the park; of Cobb's few home runs, many were of the inside-the-park variety.

Shocking as it may seem to the average fan today, home runs were not a significant part of professional baseball before 1920. In what has since become known as the "deadball" era, from 1901 to 1919, the primary offensive weapons were singles, stolen bases, and sacrifices. Home run hitting did not become commonplace until the barrel-chested George Herman "Babe" Ruth single-handedly revolutionized the sport and thrilled the nation by shattering all records for round-trippers. Since Ruth, the homer has been a staple of the game, steadily increasing in frequency in the majors until the 1960s and 1970s, when a spate of speedy runners reminded baseball strategists that power hitting was not the only way to score runs. Nowadays, both home runs and aggressive base running are prominent offensive weapons in major league baseball.

THE DEADBALL ERA

In the 1920s, Babe Ruth's home runs sparked the most radical transformation of baseball in the history of the sport. Before Ruth, from the establishment of the game's modern rules in the late 1880s through 1919, baseball was a game dominated by speed, defense, and strategy; home runs were very rare. The Bambino changed all that. To understand how one player could have such an impact on the national pastime, it is necessary to examine the pre-Ruth, pre–home run baseball era.

The first two decades of the twentieth century were, on the whole, good for professional baseball. By 1903, the success of the upstart American League had spawned the World Series, giving baseball a premier showcase that annually became the focus of attention across the nation. The success of the World Series established the structure of the major leagues. The exploits of such stars as Pittsburgh Pirates shortstop Honus Wagner, New York Giants hurler Christy Mathewson, Detroit Tigers hitting and running machine Ty Cobb, and Washington Senators flamethrower Walter Johnson—idols to boys all across the United States—further insured the preeminence of the American and National Leagues.

The brand of baseball played during the first two decades of the century was exciting, full of action and suspense—as were many of the era's pennant races. Since little had changed about the game during a thirty-year span, the players were experts at every nuance of their duties. The aggressive base running of the day, the popularity of bunting (for sacrifices and for base hits), and the expert glove work of infielders generated numerous close plays (and violent collisions) in almost every game. Fans packed the stands daily and followed the pennant races with a fervor entirely unprecedented in American sports history.

Baseball's popularity as a spectator sport was so great that twelve new and spectacular major league stadiums were opened between 1909 and 1915. The design of these stadiums contributed greatly to the Ruthian revolution of the 1920s. Before the building of these new stadiums there was rarely seating beyond the outfield, which meant there was no reason to close off the outfield at a short distance. This made hitting home runs very difficult. However, the new larger capacity stadiums contained permanent stands beyond the outfield that were near enough for fans to see the pitcher and batter. By today's standards these bleachers, as in Fenway Park's right field, are a great distance from home plate, but in 1920 they were well within reach of a muscular giant named George Herman Ruth.

In mid-1919, as World War I was being formally concluded and the troops were returning home, the United States was eagerly awaiting the World Series. What the nation got instead was a sloppy farce in which the heavily favored, extremely talented Chicago White Sox stumbled their way to defeat at the hands of the Cincinnati Reds. Late in the 1920 season, eight members of the White Sox admitted accepting money from gamblers to throw the 1919 Series. The "Black Sox" scandal stunned the United States and severely tarnished baseball's reputation. Casting a further pall over the sport in 1920 was the tragic death of Cleveland Indians star shortstop Ray Chapman during a close pennant race—he is the only major league player ever to die from being hit by a pitch. Baseball was in dire need of good news.

THE RUTHIAN BIG BANG

During the 1920 season, while disheartening rumors spread throughout major league baseball and tragedy struck on the diamond, baseball mania swept the country as never before. One player, Babe Ruth, was responsible for this paradoxical state of affairs. Over the course of the summer, the Yankees' newly acquired outfielder awed the nation with his power hitting. Ruth shattered his own record for home runs in a season (29, set in 1919) by crushing 54 round-trippers. Such a display of might was more than unparalleled—it was virtually beyond imagination; only one *team* in major league baseball produced as many as 50 homers in 1920. Ruth's Herculean batting feats and magnetic personality captured and charmed the imagination of millions of fans in what should have been baseball's darkest hour. Baseball had found a savior to lead it out of the deadball era and into the promised land.

The transformation of professional baseball from the late teens to the mid-1920s was the most dramatic and significant in the history of the sport. Over this period, the frequency of home runs, along with overall offensive production (runs per game), increased steadily; base stealing and bunting, two mainstays of deadball-era strategy, were in decline. Ruth's gargantuan blasts not only thrilled the fans but converted his peers. From the early 1920s to the present, the home run has loomed over pitchers as a constant threat.

Over the past seventy years, baseball historians and fans have debated why there was so drastic a change in the way baseball was played after 1920. The most popular explanation is that a more

Left: Legendary New York Giants hurler Christy Mathewson was one of baseball's marquee stars in the first two decades of the twentieth century. In one five-year span, from 1907 through 1911, Matty won 139 games and had an ERA below 2.00 each year. Above: George Herman Ruth was the star of the Boston Red Sox before he was sold to the New York Yankees. Since Ruth's trade, the Red Sox have gone without a World Series title (after winning three with Ruth), while the Yankees have won twenty-two.

Ruth, DiMaggio, and Mays—America's Greatest Heroes

Baseball was such an integral part of American culture during the middle decades of the twentieth century that its biggest stars—Ruth, DiMaggio, and Mays—were as renowned and revered as any celebrity or politician, including the president. These three stars, all sluggers, were not only symbols of their respective eras, but also of the nation they lived in. The public's canonization of these men was inspired by both their on-field achievements and their public personas. Babe Ruth's Olympian feats were complemented by a boisterous personality that charmed his minions throughout the Roaring Twenties, while his heartfelt compassion for the poor suited the Great Depression of the 1930s. Joe DiMaggio's stoic grace and ability to perform under pressure made him a perfect role model for a country going to war, while handsome Joe's postwar jet-setting fueled the fantasies of a newly prosperous imperial United States. Willie Mays wowed fans with his spectacular play, but it was his style— his approach to the game and to life—that set him apart from other superstars. While the struggle for racial equality was shattering the United States' postwar complacency, Willie was playing the national pastime with a contagious and unbridled joy that bypassed the mind and spoke straight to the heart. Even rival fans found themselves applauding Mays. Ultimately, the public and the print media bestowed their adoration upon Ruth, DiMaggio, and Mays because these three superstars were personable men who represented values the American people could embrace.

Since Mays' time the only American sports figure to attain such a prominent and sustained mega-celebrity status was basketball's Michael Jordan in the late 1980s and early 1990s. Jordan retired unexpectedly at the top of his game in 1993. Ironically, in the spring of 1994 he decided to pursue his childhood dream of playing major league baseball, and was awarded a tryout with the Chicago White Sox. A master of the hardwood, Jordan was humbled on the diamond and was assigned to the minor league (only AA) Birmingham Barons, where he continued to struggle. The next spring Jordan terminated his baseball career and returned to glory in the National Basketball Association.

The Sultan of Swat, Babe Ruth.

The Yankee Clipper, Joe DiMaggio.

The Say Hey Kid, Willie Mays.

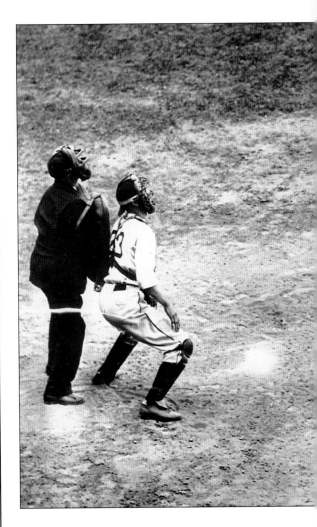

lively, tightly knit ball was introduced into the major leagues following World War I, a theory implicit in the term "deadball era." But many contemporaries, including NL President John Heydler in 1921, tested this "rabbit-ball" theory and concluded that the ball of the 1920s was no more lively than the ball used in the teens.

Another popular theory attributes the Ruthian revolution to the construction of permanent bleachers, which enclosed the outfield and, consequently, increased the likelihood of "hitting one out of the park." However, the new outfield fences were built by 1915; so why didn't the longball barrage start then? Did no one have the gumption (until Ruth) to disregard convention and take advantage of the new conditions? Or did Ruth's predecessors simply lack the ability (not the will) to launch home runs? Indeed, the veteran players who became sluggers during the power boom of the early 1920s did not hit home runs regularly until they learned how from watching Babe Ruth.

Left: From 1918 to 1920 Babe Ruth moved from the pitcher's mound to right field and from Boston to New York, where he led the Yankees to their first pennant. He also revolutionized the game with his home run hitting. Above, left: In 1930 Chicago Cubs center fielder Hack Wilson broke both the NL record for home runs, with 56, and the major league record for RBIs, with 190—both records still stand. Above, right: St. Louis Cardinals star Rogers Hornsby adjusted his hitting style after the Ruthian revolution; Hornsby, who had never hit even 10 home runs in any of his five seasons before 1920, slugged 42 in 1922.

The new enclosed outfields were a necessary precondition for the onslaught, but it took the Sultan of Swat to teach players how to hit home runs. Lessons began during the strange summer of 1920, when circumstances conspired to allow the Bambino to remake baseball in his own image.

During the 1920 season, Ruth slammed 54 home runs and became the biggest sensation in baseball history; Ray Chapman was killed when hit in the head by a pitch; and the Black Sox scandal not only brought disgrace to baseball when it erupted in September, but also destroyed a thrilling pennant race between the White Sox and Indians. The Black Sox scandal forced baseball's ruling establishment to embrace Ruth (as a boon to a beleaguered game) rather than try to curtail his record-setting offensive output, which conservatives felt made a mockery of the sport. In response to the Black Sox scandal and widespread rumors of further corruption, baseball team owners hired Kenesaw Mountain Landis as the game's

first commissioner, granting him absolute powers over the major leagues and entrusting him with reestablishing baseball's integrity. Commissioner Landis attributed Ray Chapman's death to the use of battered, darkened baseballs that hitters found difficult to see (pitchers would intentionally soil the ball for this reason). Landis mandated the use of newer, more visible baseballs. This rule not only facilitated the batter's job, but insured the use of a fresh, lively ball. Furthermore, Landis forbade pitchers to scuff up the ball in any way or throw "spitters," since such ploys darkened and damaged the ball. Thus, Landis outlawed the best pitch some hurlers had and frustrated virtually all pitchers, who found it difficult to grip shiny, new baseballs. In one fell swoop, Landis decreed a massive advantage for hitters over pitchers; a new brand of baseball was being born.

Babe Ruth swaggered into the 1921 season bearing a huge burden; owners and fans looked to Ruth to captivate audiences like the summer before. With typical nonchalance, the Babe proceeded to have a magical year. Relishing the media spotlight, Ruth set a new record with 59 home runs, and led the Yankees to their first pen-

nant. Perhaps more significantly, Ruth's influence was visible throughout the major leagues, where home runs were being hit with greater frequency.

The Bambino led a revolution in how the game was played, spawning the most popular brand of baseball to date. Before Ruth, players assumed that they could not clear the outfield fences. It took a slugger such as the Babe, whose mammoth blasts frequently traveled five hundred feet, to conquer those fences. Once Ruth's home runs had captured the public's imagination, imitation was inevitable; soon little Mel Ott was smacking 30 homers annually. Baseball had changed forever.

THE BABE AND BEYOND

Between the world wars baseball changed from a speed-oriented game to a power game. By 1921 players across the United States began emulating Ruth's uppercut swing. A dramatic increase in home runs and overall offensive production ensued. Major league recruits included more large and powerful men and fewer small, fleet-footed types. A new generation of sluggers was on deck.

Lou Gehrig (left) and Hank Greenberg were two of the greatest power hitters of all time. Gehrig ranks third in career slugging percentage, behind only Babe Ruth and Ted Williams, while Greenberg is fifth, following Jimmie Foxx. Gehrig and Greenberg were tremendous rivals. Greenberg was a native New Yorker who chose to play for the Tigers because Gehrig owned the Yankees' first base job. Greenberg then led the Tigers to the AL pennant in 1934 and 1935 before Gehrig and the Yankees won four consecutive pennants from 1936 to 1939. Following Gehrig's retirement, the Tigers rebounded to capture the flag in 1940.

The late 1920s was a golden age for baseball. The game's popularity soared to new heights and Babe Ruth attained a mythic status unrivaled in the annals of American sports. The 1927 Yankees, often called the greatest team ever, powered their way to 110 victories (with only 44 losses) and a World Series sweep. The Babe eclipsed his single-season home run record by crushing 60 homers. A new Yankees slugger, first baseman Lou Gehrig, virtually equaled Ruth's offensive production by hitting 47 home runs and collecting a record 175 RBI. In 1929, the list of sluggers who surpassed 30 homers included not only Ruth and Gehrig, but Al Simmons and Jimmie Foxx of the champion A's, Hack Wilson and Hornsby of the pennant-winning Chicago Cubs, young Mel Ott of the New York Giants, and Chuck Klein of the Philadelphia Phillies.

In 1930 offensive output reached a crescendo. The batting average for the entire National League was .303 for the season. Cubs center fielder Hack Wilson established two records that still stand today: most home runs (56) in NL history and the most RBI (190) in major league history. During the season, a consensus emerged that the ball was too lively. In 1931 a new ball was introduced and offensive production fell back to the level of the mid-1920s. Throughout the 1930s batting averages declined slowly while the number of home runs continued to increase.

During the decade of the Great Depression, the post-Ruthian generation of sluggers thrilled the nation. The Babe himself stayed in Yankees pinstripes through 1934, retiring after 1935. Fatal illness tragically cut short the career of Lou Gehrig in 1939, though he still retired as the game's second-greatest power hitter. Jimmie Foxx of the A's and Red Sox emerged as the game's most prolific slugger by slamming 415 home runs across the decade, including 58 in 1932. Mel Ott was the most prolific power hitter in the senior circuit during the 1930s. With five games remaining in the 1938 season the Detroit Tigers' Hank Greenberg blasted his 58th homer, two shy of Ruth's record. With the nation's attention focused on him, Greenberg failed to hit another home run. In 1941, World War II interrupted the careers of many great players including Greenberg and young sluggers Joe DiMaggio and Ted Williams. By the outbreak of the war, the home run was firmly established as baseball's most celebrated play.

POSTWAR BASEBALL: AN ERA OF SLUGGERS

From the end of World War II until the mid-1960s, home run hitting dominated baseball as never before or since. Throughout the 1950s, the prevailing approach to scoring runs was to get men on base and then hit a home run. Muscle men who specialized in the longball and little else, such as Ted Kluszewski, Rocky Colavito, and Ralph Kiner, were prototypical postwar ballplayers. Kiner was the best of the lot, leading the National League in home runs a record seven consecutive times, twice hitting more than 50 home runs in a season and batting over .300 four times. The era had some great all-around hitters, such as Ted Williams, Stan Musial, and three exceptional New York center fielders: Duke Snider, Mickey Mantle, and Willie Mays. Talented singles hitters and defensive wizards became rarities since all players were expected to contribute the occasional three-run homer.

In the 1960s home runs continued to dominate offensive strategy, though things began to change. Never before or since have so many great career sluggers played at the same time: Mays, Mantle, Eddie Mathews, Ernie Banks, Henry Aaron, Harmon Killebrew, Frank Robinson, and Willie McCovey—more than half the players who have hit 500 or more career home runs—were all in their prime during the 1960s. In 1961 New York Yankee Roger Maris surpassed Ruth's single-season record by crushing his 61st home run during the final game of the season. When home run totals remained high during the 1962 season, the Baseball Rules Committee voted to expand the strike zone.

Soon pitchers began retiring the less-talented power hitters with increasing regularity. In 1961 players had hit a record 1.92 home runs per game; by 1967 the average was down to 1.42. The resultant decrease in offense placed a greater emphasis on defense, which led to the return of small, quick, contact-hitting defensive specialists. In 1968, the "year of the pitcher," offense was so low—the home run average plummeted to 1.23 per game—that the Rules Committee reduced the strike zone and shortened the pitcher's mound. Offensive production and home run totals rebounded the next year.

In 1970, home run hitting reached another peak. In 1920, when Ruth shattered all previous power-hitting records, there were .51 homers per

From the late 1940s through the early 1960s, home run hitting dominated baseball. From television's *Home Run Derby*, in which major league stars competed in a home run hitting tournament, to pick up games on the sandlots of the United States, hitting the long ball personified the national pastime throughout this era. The great hitters of the time were line drive hitters who knew how to lift the ball over the fence, including Frank Robinson (top), being greeted by Reds muscle man Ted Kluszewski following a home run; Willie McCovey (above, left) of the Giants; and Ted Williams (above, right) of the Red Sox.

game. The average rose to 1.27 for the watershed 1930 season. By 1950 fans could expect 1.67 home runs per game. In 1970 the average was up to 1.76—an amazing increase in two years. However, the 1960s, like the teens, was a decade of stadium construction. In the 1970s a new brand of baseball emerged in the new venues, one that reversed the fifty-year trend towards more home runs.

THE 1970s AND BEYOND

Baseball changed more dramatically in the 1970s than in any decade since the 1920s. Fittingly, the most significant changes were reversals of trends that began in the 1920s: base stealing and speed reemerged as major forces in the 1970s, and home run hitting declined. Much as in the 1920s, the evolution of baseball in the 1970s was partly due to players adapting to their new confines. The new stadiums of the 1960s and 1970s were often vast (and never small). A 1959 rule set minimum boundaries for new parks at 325 feet down each foul line and 400 feet to center; there would be no more friendly porches like right field in Yankee Stadium (315 feet). By 1976, fifteen of the twenty-four major league stadiums were built after the ordinance. In many cities, home runs were bound to decrease. By 1975, the home runs per game average was down to 1.39.

Also, the widespread installation of Astroturf in the early 1970s (a cost-cutting measure adopted by nine owners) contributed to the de-emphasis of power. An artificial surface rewards line drive hitters since it does not slow down a bouncing ball as much as natural grass. The carpet increases the value of small, speedy players who can stretch line drives into extra bases on offense and run down balls more effectively on defense.

On the subject of speed, the stolen base continued a comeback that actually began in the 1960s. Maury Wills stole a record 104 bases for the Los Angeles Dodgers in 1962, which was also the team's first year in cavernous Dodger Stadium. Still, few teams featured base-stealing threats at the start of the 1970s. However, both the A's dynasty of the early 1970s and the world-champion (Cincinnati) Big Red Machine of that decade combined speed with power. By 1980, most teams had a few speedsters on their rosters.

By the early 1980s the new revolution was complete, and most teams were striving for

Mike Schmidt of the Philadelphia Phillies was the premier home run hitter in baseball during the late 1970s and 1980s. While many teams began to construct their attacks around speed instead of power during this time, Schmidt's mix of long balls, searing line drives, and patience at the plate made him the most potent offensive force in baseball during his prime. In 1980 Schmidt and pitching great Steve Carlton led the Phillies to their only world championship.

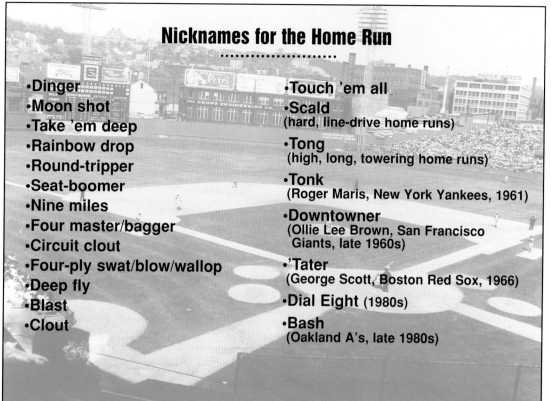

Nicknames for the Home Run

- •Dinger
- •Moon shot
- •Take 'em deep
- •Rainbow drop
- •Round-tripper
- •Seat-boomer
- •Nine miles
- •Four master/bagger
- •Circuit clout
- •Four-ply swat/blow/wallop
- •Deep fly
- •Blast
- •Clout

- •Touch 'em all
- •Scald
  (hard, line-drive home runs)
- •Tong
  (high, long, towering home runs)
- •Tonk
  (Roger Maris, New York Yankees, 1961)
- •Downtowner
  (Ollie Lee Brown, San Francisco
  Giants, late 1960s)
- •'Tater
  (George Scott, Boston Red Sox, 1966)
- •Dial Eight (1980s)
- •Bash
  (Oakland A's, late 1980s)

balanced attacks, with speed at the top of the batting order and power in the middle. Some teams—from smaller, older parks with natural grass, like the Tigers and Red Sox—remained loyal to the power-only baseball of the 1950s. Tenants of vast stadiums, like the Cardinals and Astros, seemed like throwbacks to the deadball era with their speed-oriented, slap-hitting attacks. During the 1970s and 1980s, sluggers like Reggie Jackson and Mike Schmidt shared the spotlight with speedsters like Lou Brock and singles hitters like Rod Carew and Pete Rose.

In the late 1980s and early 1990s a new generation of sluggers headed by Jose Canseco, Barry Bonds, and Ken Griffey, Jr., exploded on the baseball scene. Products of the 1970s and 1980s, these new sluggers combined speed and power. They recalled the likes of Willie Mays and Henry Aaron, players who could do it all: field, hit for power and average, and steal bases. Baseball in the 1990s not only combines the speed and finesse of the deadball era with the slugging of home runs, but also features the talents of a new wave of transcendent players whose accomplishments may someday rival those of the greatest stars from the annals of the national pastime.

Top, left: Jose Canseco completes his mammoth swing and follows the flight of the ball towards the bleachers. When Canseco came up with the A's in the 1980s he was an all-around threat, able to hit for average and power and to steal bases; in recent years his game has become more one-dimensional, and he is now primarily a home run hitter. Top, right: Cincinnati's Crosley Field in the 1950s. Above: Barry Bonds established himself as baseball's best player during his days with the Pittsburgh Pirates in the late 1980s. Now with the San Francisco Giants, Bonds remains a legitimate triple-crown threat and is one of many contemporary players who could threaten Roger Maris' single-season home run record.

CHAPTER TWO

The Big Three: Ruth, Mays, and Aaron

Of all major league sluggers, only three men ever belted more than 600 home runs during their careers: Babe Ruth, Willie Mays, and Henry Aaron. Not surprisingly, these three men are among the best-known figures in both sport lore and history in general.

The Babe achieved his career total without precedent, breaking the all-time record (120 home runs) in his third year as an outfielder. Mays and Aaron spent significant portions of their storied careers chasing Ruth's mark of 714 home runs, baseball's most celebrated record. Mays' prodigious home run production preceded Aaron's by a few years, which allowed Hammerin' Hank to approach the Babe's record in relative obscurity. Mays, handicapped by the two seasons he missed to military service early in his career, fell short of the Babe; in 1972, Aaron surpassed Mays. For the next two years, Aaron played under unprecedented media scrutiny as he closed in on 714. He broke Ruth's record during the first week of the 1974 season. Aaron finished his career with 755 home runs, 41 more than Ruth; of course, Aaron had 3,965 more career at-bats than the Babe. No player has since threatened Aaron's mark, and no active player seems within range today. Aaron's humble words from 1974 capture the essence of the recordholder's outlook on his relation to the Babe: "The legend of Babe Ruth is indestructible. It won't matter whether I hit 800 homers...there will never be another Babe Ruth as far as the baseball public is concerned. And someday, some young guy will come along and hit 850 home runs and I'll be just another home run hitter whose record was broken."

Throughout Willie Mays' prime in the 1960s, fans and journalists alike speculated whether the Say Hey Kid would eclipse Babe Ruth's career home run total, the most prestigious record in all of professional U.S. sports. Undaunted by such speculation, Mays just kept being Mays; that is, he played baseball better, and with more charisma, than anyone else.

BABE RUTH

The Babe, the Bambino, the Sultan of Swat—the one and only Babe Ruth remains to this day the United States' greatest sporting legend. A poorly educated orphan who began his major league career as a pitcher, Babe Ruth's titanic home runs and magnetic personality transformed him into the greatest idol of his day and the cigar-smoking personification of baseball the entire world over.

George Herman Ruth, Jr., was born in Baltimore, Maryland, on February 6, 1895, to

saloonkeepers George and Katherine Ruth. Young George spent his early years without much supervision, learning the way of the streets and adopting the mannerisms of the saloon's clientele. Branded "incorrigible" by the age of seven, the tobacco-chewing child was sent to St. Mary's Orphanage by his parents. At St. Mary's, the Xaverian priests taught the orphans baseball. By his teens, Ruth was the star catcher and first baseman for the St. Mary's Industrial School team. At the age of nineteen, George, who was six-foot-two and weighed around two hundred pounds, tried out for the prestigious minor league Baltimore Orioles. Owner Jack Dunn was impressed by Ruth and became his legal guardian so that the youngster could play for the Orioles. Dunn converted the powerful, left-handed Ruth into a pitcher.

The Babe possessed a blinding fastball and made an instant impact on the Orioles, posting a complete game shutout in his first professional appearance. Because of his age, the Oriole players dubbed him "Babe." His star rose so quickly that Dunn soon sold Ruth to the major league Boston Red Sox. After a few outings with Boston, Ruth was optioned to the Providence team, which was in the same league as the Orioles. Ruth compiled a 22-9 record for Baltimore and Providence in 1914, the best record in the league. At the end of the season, Ruth returned to Boston, where he won two games. At nineteen Babe Ruth was finished with the minor leagues. He only hit one home run in the minors, a clout that was overshadowed by the shutout Ruth threw in the same game.

In 1915 Ruth became a part of a great pennant-winning pitching staff. Babe won 18 and lost

Left: Babe Ruth began his major league career as a pitcher for the Red Sox and was no ordinary hurler. Ruth was Boston's ace from 1916 through 1918 and starred in World Series victories in 1916 and 1918. Ruth possessed a blazing fastball, quality breaking stuff, and good control. His career ERA of 2.28 is the tenth-lowest total in major league history. Above: Babe Ruth signs baseballs handed to him by a security guard, while his teammates look on from the Yankee dugout. In 1920 Ruth became the biggest star in the biggest city and, soon after, across the rest of the nation as well. Note that Ruth, who batted and threw with his left hand, wrote with his right.

only 8 games for the Red Sox. However, Ruth only appeared as a pinch-hitter in the World Series, which Boston won. The Red Sox recognized Ruth's talent as a slugger as he led the team with 4 homers in only 92 at-bats. His first major league home run occurred on May 6, 1915, at New York's Polo Grounds, where he sent Yankee Jack Warhop's pitch into the right-field upper deck.

In 1916 the young Babe emerged as the ace of another Red Sox pennant-winning team, going 23-12 with a league-leading 1.75 ERA. The Babe's home run output, however, fell to 3. In the World Series, Ruth started the second game and, after giving up a run in the first inning, pitched thirteen consecutive scoreless innings until the Red Sox managed a 2-1 victory in the fourteenth. The BoSox defeated Brooklyn four games to one to capture their second straight title.

The Red Sox failed to win the American League in 1917, though Ruth had another great year with 24 wins, 13 losses, and a 2.02 ERA. Though he hit only two home runs, his .325 batting average was his best yet. In 1918 Red Sox manager Ed Barrow decided to try to capitalize on Ruth's hitting skill and, in an unprecedented maneuver for the major leagues, split Ruth's playing time between the outfield, first base, and the pitcher's mound. Ruth started 59 games in the outfield and 13 at first base, and compiled a 13-7 record as a pitcher. Ruth hit .300 and clubbed 11 home runs to tie for the league lead, though he batted only 317 times. In the 1918 World Series Ruth's duties were restricted to starting pitching. Babe pitched a shutout in Game One, and began Game Four with seven shutout innings that led to a 3-2 victory. Babe and the BoSox won their third Series title in four years. Across 1916 and 1918, Ruth strung together 29.67 consecutive scoreless innings in the World Series, a record that stood until 1961. Ruth's overall pitching record in the Fall Classic was 3-0 with a 0.87 ERA, still the lowest in Series history.

The year 1919 was Ruth's last as a regular pitcher, and he went 9-5 with a 2.97 ERA. In later years the Yankees would start Ruth as pitcher toward the end of the year if the pinstripes had been eliminated from the pennant race and wanted to boost attendance. As a Yankee Ruth won all five of his pitching starts and finished with a career record of 94-46 and a 2.28 ERA.

By mid-1919, when it was clear the Red Sox had no chance to repeat as pennant winners, Manager Ed Barrow made Ruth a starting outfielder. On July 5 Ruth responded with his first-ever 2–home run game. By mid-July he had equaled his previous season's total of 11 home runs. Ruth set his sights on the record book: the AL record was 16, set by the A's Ralph Seybold in 1902. The major league mark was 24, set by Clifford (Gavvy) Cravath of the Phillies in 1915. The Washington Senators' John Freeman had hit 25 in 1899, but the all-time high was by the Chicago White Sox's Edward Williamson, who belted 27 in 1884 (he hit 25 home runs over the 215-foot right-field fence at his home field, the Congress Street Grounds, and only 2 on the road).

Babe Ruth crosses home plate after slugging his record-breaking 60th home run of 1927 on the last day of the season. First to congratulate the Babe is on-deck hitter Lou Gehrig, who had battled Ruth for the league lead in homers through mid-August.

On August 14 Ruth hit number 17, setting an AL record. His 20th home run was his fourth grand slam of the year, which remained a record for one season until Ernie Banks hit five in 1955. Newspapers across the United States began to print a special box devoted to Ruth's pursuit of Williamson. Fans throughout the American League packed the stands to see the great home run slugger. Ruth had 23 homers by Labor Day, and hit number 25 within a week. On September 20, in the ninth inning of the second game of a double-header, Ruth hit his 27th home run, the game winner. A few days later he set the new record with a massive blow over the roof at the Polo Grounds. He finished the year with 29 home runs; the final blast was his first ever in Washington. Ruth had homered in every AL park.

After the 1919 season the financially strapped Red Sox made the most celebrated (or infamous, depending on perspective) sale in baseball history: they sent Babe Ruth to the New York Yankees in exchange for $100,000 and a $300,000 loan. Legend has it that the sale cast a spell, known as the "curse of the Bambino," over the Red Sox that is still in effect: the BoSox have not won a World Series since 1918. In contrast, the Yankees have won 22 World Series since Ruth joined their ranks.

In 1920 Ruth rewrote the record book on power hitting, smashing 54 home runs, hitting .376, driving in 137 RBI, and compiling a slugging percentage of .847, a mark that remains the single-season record. At a time when professional baseball was in the midst of a huge crisis that threatened to discredit the national pastime in the eyes of its fans, Ruth captured the imagination of the United States like no baseball player had before him. In 1921 Ruth once again captivated the land as he honed in on his home run total from the previous year. Not only did he eclipse his record with 59 home runs, but he batted .378 and set a new record with 171 RBI. On June 10, 1921, Ruth hit his 120th career home run, breaking the all-time record held by Gavvy Cravath. In 1921 Ruth also led the Yankees to their first pennant ever, though the New York Giants defeated them in the World Series.

Ruth missed part of the 1922 season when Commissioner Landis suspended him for barnstorming (touring the country) in the off-season, an activity deemed inappropriate for major league stars. Nevertheless, Ruth regained his form late in the season and the Yankees won the pennant for the second time; once again the Giants crushed them in the Series, 4-0. In 1923, however, the Yankees gained revenge on their hometown rivals. Yankee Stadium opened in the Bronx in 1923, across the Harlem River from the Polo Grounds, where the Yankees had never been more than the Giants' tenants. Ruth homered in the inaugural game at the new stadium, which the media christened "the house that Ruth built." Ruth hit a career high .393 with 41 home runs in 1923, and the Yankees won their third straight pennant. In the Series the Yankees defeated the Giants 4-2 to win their first world title.

By the mid-1920s Ruth had become not only baseball's but the United States' greatest hero. The Roaring Twenties was an era of new-found prosperity, grand spectacles, and fun; Ruth's joyous demeanor and heroic feats seemed to embody the age. The Babe approached life with reckless abandon and good humor, eating, drinking, and living life to excess. Also, Ruth was tremendously kindhearted; children were more important to the Babe than were the heads of state who flocked to have their picture taken with him. No matter the occasion or the makeup of the crowd, Ruth charmed his legions; he was a hero for all peoples (except, of course, opposing pitchers).

Ruth did not look like a great athlete. He was pigeon-toed and had spindly legs and a huge, broad torso. Yet Ruth was a very good right fielder and an excellent baserunner (he stole 123 bases). In the batter's box he was in a league by himself. Ruth stood with his feet close together, with his right (front) foot about two inches closer to the plate than his left foot. He stood somewhat deep in the batter's box and took a big stride forward, planting his back leg firmly. He held the bat at the bottom of its length, the knob actually in his right hand. He brought the bat through the strike zone with a slight uppercut, snapping his wrists at the moment of impact. The force of his swing was

Sadaharu Oh

The most prolific home run hitter in the history of professional baseball was neither Ruth nor Henry Aaron, but Sadaharu Oh. In a career that spanned from 1958 to 1980 Oh amassed 868 career round-trippers for the Tokyo Giants of the Japanese League. A left-handed first baseman standing five-foot-ten and weighing 174 pounds, Oh choked up on the bat and used a high leg kick to time a smooth and powerful swing. Oh won back-to-back triple crowns in 1973 and 1974, nine MVP awards, fifteen home run crowns, 13 RBI titles, and four batting titles; he also spent eighteen consecutive years leading his league in walks. Oh's teams dominated Japanese baseball from the mid-1960s through the early 1970s. Since Oh's slugging feats were accomplished in stadiums considerably smaller than those in the United States it is generally assumed that he would not have compiled as many home runs in the states (though he would have had more opportunities to hit homers, since the American season has 162 games while the Japanese has only 120). American major leaguers who played against Oh in exhibitions agreed that the lifetime .301 hitter would have been a star in the United States, though he probably would not have challenged Aaron's home run record.

Top: Sadaharu Oh blasts a ball towards the right-field bleachers in his 1974 home run derby versus Henry Aaron. The pitcher is Joe Pignatano of the New York Mets. Above: Though he became renowned as Japan's greatest baseball star, Oh remained a modest man and a hardworking player.

In late 1974 Oh competed against Henry Aaron in a home run derby. Both sluggers would get to hit twenty fair balls, thrown by the batting practice pitcher of their choice. The venue was Tokyo's Korakuen Stadium. Aaron was confident, even though Oh was in his prime and Hank was well past his. The derby was broken down into four rounds, five hits for each man per round. Oh led 3-2 after round one, and then belted 3 more homers in round two. Then Aaron caught fire, hitting 4 straight to the seats to tie the score 6-6 after two rounds. After Aaron outslugged Oh 3-1 in round three, Oh only managed to tie up the score at 9-9 in the top of the fourth. Aaron won the contest, 10-9, with his third hit of the final frame; then Aaron smiled, turned, and walked away from home plate.

so great that he often lost his balance if he missed; but when he made contact, Ruth's swing was a display of grace and effortless power. Ruth summarized both his swing and his approach to life in one fell swoop:

"How to hit home runs: I swing as hard as I can, and I try to swing right through the ball. In boxing, your fist usually stops when you hit a man, but it's possible to hit so hard that your fist doesn't stop. I try to follow through in the same way. The harder you grip the bat, the more you can swing it through the ball, and the farther the ball will go. I swing big, with everything I've got. I hit big or I miss big. I like to live as big as I can."

Ruth played for the Yankees until 1934, winning four more pennants and three more World Series titles. The 1927 Yankees team, which won 110 games and swept the Series, has become renowned as the greatest team ever. Ruth retired after playing the 1935 season with the Boston Braves. He won or shared twelve home run titles on the way to slamming 714 career home runs. Ruth averaged more home runs per at-bat than any player in major league history. Thus, his status as baseball's greatest slugger has statistical as well as mythical substance.

Babe Ruth died of cancer on August 16, 1948. More than a year earlier, on April 27, 1947, the Yankees honored the already seriously ill legend with "Babe Ruth Day" at Yankee Stadium. The sellout crowd of 58,339 gave the Babe the longest standing ovation in sports history. Barely able to speak, Ruth walked up to the microphone and in a raspy whisper said, "There's been so many lovely things said about me, I'm glad I had the opportunity to thank everybody. Thank you." Following his death, Ruth lay in state under the rotunda at Yankee Stadium, where over 100,000 fans filed past his coffin to pay their last respects to the Bambino, the greatest baseball player who ever lived.

WILLIE MAYS

Willie Mays, like Babe Ruth and Joe DiMaggio, was one of baseball's defining personalities, its greatest star during his career. Aaron ultimately hit more home runs and Mantle won more championships than Mays, but the Say Hey Kid played with a flair that captivated fans and made him baseball's supreme idol for twenty years.

Above: Willie Mays has just made the most famous catch in baseball history, on a ball hit by Cleveland Indian Vic Wertz during the first game of the 1954 World Series; he is beginning to turn and throw the ball back to the infield to keep the lead runner from scoring. Willie's catch in the top of the eighth inning kept the score tied 2-2 and allowed the Giants to go on to win the game in extra innings. Note the "483 feet" sign to Mays' left; he caught the ball over his shoulder in the deepest part of the Polo Grounds, which had the largest center field in the majors.

Willie Mays was born in Westfield, Alabama, on May 6, 1931, the son of steel-mill worker William Mays and his wife, Ann. Willie was raised by his aunt Sarah in Fairfield, Alabama, because his parents were divorced shortly after his birth. Willie attended Fairfield Industrial High School, where he excelled in many sports, especially baseball. He began playing ball professionally at the age of seventeen with the Birmingham Barons of the Negro Leagues. The New York Giants purchased the contract of the five-foot-ten-and-one-half-inch, 170-pound, right-handed outfielder in 1950 and assigned him to Trenton.

In the spring of 1951, the Giants sent Mays to their AAA affiliate in Minneapolis, one stop short of the big leagues. The legend of Willie Mays began that spring in Minnesota. The fans adored him and sang his praises endlessly; no one could hit, field, run, or throw like Willie Mays. The Giants called Mays up to the majors after he played only 35 games for Minneapolis; Willie was batting .477 at the time. The owner of the Giants placed an advertisement in the Minnesota papers apologizing for taking Mays away.

The New York team that Mays joined was destined for baseball immortality, though no one knew

Top, from left to right: Willie Mays tracks down a line drive to deep right center field in his days with the New York Giants. Above: Mays completes his follow-through as the catcher and umpire glance up at the ball rocketing towards the bleachers. Leo Durocher, legendary manager of the Giants, once said, "There are five things that Willie Mays can do better than anyone else in the history of the game—run, throw, catch, hit, and hit with power."

it at the time. Leo Durocher's Giants had begun the season losing 12 of 14 games. The team fared better after that, but remained mired in the second division until Mays joined the team on May 25 for a three-game series in Philadelphia. The Giants swept the Phillies. Though Willie had failed to get a hit in that series, on the train back to New York manager Durocher declared that "Mays can take us all the way." Journalists covering the Giants at the time swore that Mays' presence transformed his teammates; Mays enjoyed playing baseball so much that it rubbed off on the other Giants. In the first game back at the Polo Grounds, Mays crushed a first-inning three-run homer off pitching great Warren Spahn that sailed over the left-field roof.

By August 11, 1951, the Giants had moved up to second place, but remained 13.5 games behind their hated rivals, the Brooklyn Dodgers. The Giants then won 16 straight games, and ultimately won 37 of 44 to finish in a tie with the Dodgers for first place. The Giants won the pennant on Bobby Thomson's three-run ninth-inning home run in the third and decisive playoff game. Mays won NL Rookie of the Year honors. He only hit .274 with 20 home runs, but his enthusiastic presence, combined with his hitting and spectacular fielding, had catapulted the Giants into pennant contention.

After serving in the U.S. Army for most of the 1952 season and all of 1953, Mays returned to the Giants in 1954. Picking up where he left off, Willie led the Giants back to the World Series. The Say Hey Kid, as Willie was known because of the cheerful "say hey" greeting he used with friends and strangers alike, had matured as a batter. He topped the National League with a .345 average while smashing 41 home runs and driving in 110 runs. Mays was voted the National League MVP for the season.

Josh Gibson

Josh Gibson was the most feared slugger in the history of the Negro Leagues. Born in Georgia in 1911, Gibson played not only in the Negro Leagues from 1930 to 1946, but also in Latin-American circuits during the middle of his career. A top-flight defensive catcher, Gibson teamed with Satchel Paige on the Pittsburgh Crawfords in the mid-1930s to form perhaps the greatest battery in baseball history. Many of Gibson's home runs were of legendary proportions. The most famous homer came on September 27, 1930, during the Negro League Playoff, when Gibson hit a huge home run that, according to some observers (accounts vary), was the only ball ever hit entirely out of Yankee Stadium—a feat never accomplished by Ruth, Mantle, or any other slugger. Tragically, Gibson died of a brain tumor in January 1947, a mere three months before Jackie Robinson's debut with the Brooklyn Dodgers signaled the beginning of the end of baseball's segregation.

Estimates of Gibson's career home run total range from 250 to 900. However, using only the statistics from well-documented games, Gibson powered 236 home runs in 3,189 at-bats (while batting .362). At that home run–to–at-bat ratio he would have hit 622 home runs had he batted as often as Babe Ruth, and he would have smashed an astounding 996 home runs had he had as many official at-bats as Henry Aaron. However, in exhibitions in which he faced major league hurlers, Gibson only connected for 1 home run in 61 attempts, though he batted .426. Perhaps his power numbers would have been lower in the majors; perhaps not. There is no doubt, though, that Josh Gibson was one of the greatest hitters of all time.

Josh Gibson bats for the Homestead Grays. Gibson's powerful build and strong grip keyed an awesome swing that generated some of the longest home runs ever hit.

In the World Series, the Giants played the heavily favored Cleveland Indians, who had set a new AL record for the most games won in a single season. However, the Giants had a secret weapon—Willie Mays. In the first game, he made the most memorable defensive play in World Series history. The game was tied 2-2 in the eighth inning when the Indians' first two batters reached base. The next hitter, slugger Vic Wertz, crushed a ball 460 feet to dead center field, well beyond the fence of every major league stadium—except New York's Polo Grounds. Mays turned at the crack of the bat and sprinted, head down, toward deepest center field. Running at full speed, Mays gave the slightest peek over his left shoulder just as the ball was falling to earth and made the catch over his shoulder, on the run with his back to home plate. In one fluid motion, he turned and threw a rifle shot back to the infield so that the lead runner was unable to score. The crowd, Cleveland, and the entire nation were stunned. The Giants went on to win the game in extra innings, and swept the Indians in the Series 4-0.

At the age of twenty-three, Willie Mays had become the United States' newest idol. He appeared on the *Ed Sullivan Show* and graced the cover of *Time* magazine. Journalists and fans alike raised the question: was he the greatest ever? He hit for average and power, ran the bases with lightning speed, had a great arm, and played the outfield like no one ever had before. Mays also brought a style all his own to the game that was in evidence with every graceful basket catch. (Instead of catching fly balls above his head like other outfielders, Mays caught the ball underhand at waist level.) Mays had charmed New York City; word spread that between games he often played stickball with young kids on the streets of Harlem. Willie Mays' love for baseball could not be restricted to the fields of the major leagues; likewise, the adoration of the New York fans knew no bounds.

In 1955 Mays hit 51 homers to lead the league for the first time. The next year the Say Hey Kid led the National League in stolen bases (as he did for three years after that). He became the first player ever to steal 30 bases and hit 30 homers in a season (in 1956 and again in 1957), and remains the only player ever to hit 50 home runs and steal 20 bases in a season (in 1955). Mays could do it all. Fans across the National League cheered him on the bases, rooted for him at the plate, and reveled in his spectacular defense. Babe Ruth was the only player ever to rival Mays in popularity, but the Sultan of Swat was a one-dimensional attraction compared to Mays. The San Francisco Giants were the leading road attraction in Major League Baseball from 1958 to 1971; the New York Mets became the top draw in 1972, when Willie Mays was traded from the Giants to the Mets.

From 1955 through 1965, Willie Mays crushed 462 home runs. At the age of thirty-four, Mays had 527 career home runs and was ahead of the pace that Aaron would have at the same age (consider, too, that Mays had missed two years in the armed services). However, following 1965 Mays' home run production fell off. Whereas Aaron hit 44, 38, 47, 34, and 40 home runs in the seasons after he was 34 years old, Mays only hit 37, 22, 23, 13, and 28. Nevertheless, if Mays had not lost nearly two full years, it's likely that he would have hit the 54 home runs separating him from the Babe. Mays would have broken the Babe's record and reveled in the glory of that moment; then Aaron would have eclipsed Mays. However, it didn't happen that way, and Mays had to settle for 660 career home runs and a legacy worthy of an American legend.

HENRY AARON

For the majority of his playing days, Henry Aaron performed brilliantly in relative obscurity. Every baseball fan knew that Aaron was an all-around superstar who hit for average and power, ran the bases swiftly, and played the outfield superbly, but he wasn't front-page news. Of course, Aaron entered the spotlight when his team won two pennants and a World Series in the late 1950s, but Milwaukee was a small city and Aaron garnered few national headlines once the Braves stopped contending for championships. Then, in 1969 some sportswriters noticed that Aaron, who had hit for power consistently but not spectacularly for fifteen seasons (never more than 47 home runs, never fewer than 24), had a good shot at surpassing the most hallowed record in all of baseball, Babe Ruth's career home run total of 714. The writers pointed out that Aaron was only thirty-five years old, in great shape, still hitting homers with regularity, and had already passed 500 career homers. His obscurity was coming to an end.

Throughout the 1960s Hank Aaron played magnificently for the Milwaukee and Atlanta Braves. Unlike Willie Mays, who began his career in the media capital of the world and played for a perennial contender, Aaron—like the Braves—rarely entered the national spotlight. However, as Aaron's home run total grew he began to receive more and more attention and acknowledgment from fans and the press.

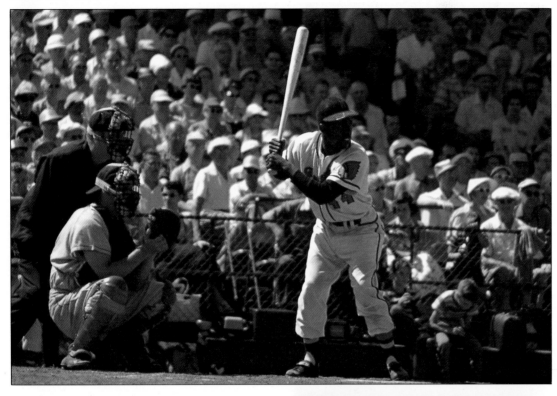

Henry Aaron was born on February 5, 1934, in Mobile, Alabama, the third of eight children born to Herbert and Estille Aaron. Henry's father was a rivet-buckler for the Alabama Shipyard Company. Since money was tight during the Depression, young Henry helped his family survive by delivering ice around Mobile. When he wasn't working, he was either playing ball or watching grown-ups play ball. In his grammar-school days, Henry played catcher on a team in a recreational league. The quiet, hardworking boy loved baseball. However, each of the two segregated high schools Henry attended didn't have enough money to field a baseball team, so Henry had to settle for softball. Fortunately, Henry made the semipro Mobile Black Bears during his junior year. At the end of the season, the Black Bears played the barnstorming Indianapolis Clowns of the Negro Leagues, and the young Henry Aaron impressed the Clowns so much that they offered him the opportunity to play professional ball with them during the next season.

Hank Aaron played for the Indianapolis Clowns during the 1951 season and led the Negro Leagues in hitting with a miraculous .467 average. By the early 1950s major league scouts were swarming all around Negro League games, and in 1952 the Giants and the Braves expressed interest

in signing Aaron, who was a shortstop at the time. After some deliberation, the Clowns told the Braves either to sign Aaron immediately or get lost. The next day Henry was $2,500 richer and on a train to Eau Claire, Wisconsin, for a thirty-day tryout with the Braves' organization. In 87 games in the Northern League, Aaron batted .336 with 9 home runs and 61 RBI. The performance was good enough to earn Aaron a promotion to AAA for the 1953 season. At Jacksonville Henry Aaron made a smooth transition from shortstop to second base, batting .362, knocking in 125 runs, and slamming 22 round-trippers to win the Sally League MVP trophy.

Aaron had heard rumors that the Braves planned to use him in the outfield, so he spent the winter learning a new position in the Puerto Rican Winter League. Indeed, Aaron became the Braves' starting right fielder in 1954, and he performed exceedingly well: he hit .280 with 13 home runs and 69 RBI. Then he fractured his right ankle sliding into third base on September 5, effectively ending his season.

Aaron had impressed his teammates with his skills and his ability to learn quickly during his inaugural season, but the injury left doubts in his mind. Years later he recalled, "People say I look like I never worry but that isn't true. I worried a lot before, during and after my rookie year." He bounced back from the injury and improved his offensive production, batting .314, hitting 27 homers, and driving in 106 runs in 1955. In his third season, 1956, Aaron won the first of his three batting titles with a .328 average; he also had 26 home runs and 92 RBI.

In 1956 the Braves lost the pennant to the Dodgers in the last week of the season, but the next year things were different. In 1957 the Braves moved up to the next level. The Braves team featured the great starting pitching of veterans Warren Spahn and Lew Burdette, a strong double-play combination of Johnny Logan and Red Schoendienst, power-hitting catcher Del Crandall, and a murderers' row in the middle of the order featuring sluggers Aaron, Eddie

Above, left: Aaron once said, "It may sound silly, but I don't hear a thing when I'm at bat. Someone can be standing hollering right at the dugout, but I don't hear it. I'm concentrating on the pitcher."
Left: Hammerin' Hank's Milwaukee Braves teammates carry him off the field after he clinched the 1957 pennant with a dramatic extra-inning home run.

Mathews, and Joe Adcock. The Braves clinched the pennant with a week left in the season on a dramatic bottom-of-the-eleventh-inning blast by Hank Aaron. Hammerin' Hank had his best season yet, batting .322 and leading the league with 44 home runs and 132 RBI. The Braves won the World Series in seven games. Fittingly Henry Aaron was voted the NL MVP.

Aaron was baseball's quiet superstar, recognized during the Braves' reign atop the majors as one of the two best all-around baseball players (with Willie Mays). Years later Eddie Mathews had this to say about Aaron in the late 1950s: "He was so obviously superior to everyone else that there was no sense talking about it." Pitching great Curt Simmons noted that "throwing a fast ball by Henry Aaron is like trying to sneak the sun past a rooster." Commentary on Aaron's hitting focused on the strength of his wrists; Milwaukee manager Fred Haney told reporters, "He operates the same way [Rogers] Hornsby did, just meeting the ball wherever it's pitched and counting on his wrist power to give it a ride." Eddie Mathews added this observation on Aaron the batter and man: "Hank has his weight on his front foot instead of his back foot when he connects and that's a flaw in any batting textbook. But it also tells you something about Hank. He has done it all for himself. No hitting instructor has ever been able to help him."

In 1958 the Braves won the NL pennant again, and Aaron contributed another sterling season, slugging 30 home runs, collecting 95 RBI, and hitting .326. However, the Yankees exacted their revenge, overcoming a 3-1 deficit in games to win the Series in seven. The 1958 season marked Aaron's last appearance in the Fall Classic. Aaron had performed marvelously over

Aaron completes the most anticipated swing in major league history, number 715. The significance of the event transcended the sport: only twenty-seven years after Jackie Robinson broke through the major league color barrier, a black man eclipsed the most hallowed record in all of American sports, and he did it in the heart of the recently desegregated South. While Aaron received a steady stream of hate mail and even some racially motivated death threats from around the country, Atlanta unequivocally embraced Aaron. Calm and soft-spoken throughout the ordeal, Aaron proved himself to be a true hero.

the two Series versus the Yankees, batting .364, belting 3 home runs (all in 1957), and posting 9 RBI. In 1959 the Braves tied for the top spot in the National League, but lost in a playoff to the Dodgers. In 1960 the Braves finished in second, behind the Pirates, and then fell out of contention for most of the 1960s. Aaron did appear again in post season play in 1969, when the Braves won the NL West, but they were swept by the "miracle" Mets in the League Championship Series.

Thus, throughout the 1960s Aaron played for a team that received little attention. By 1968 Aaron had led the National League in both

homers and RBI four times, and in batting average twice. He had never sustained an injury that seriously shortened a season. By the beginning of the 1969 season, Aaron had compiled 510 home runs. Still, it would take unprecedented home run production past the age of thirty-five for Aaron to catch Ruth. Then the Braves moved to Atlanta. One factor in Aaron's favor was that after spending most of his career playing his home games in Milwaukee County Stadium—a notoriously bad park for home run hitters—Atlanta's Folsom County Stadium was conducive to home run hitting. Over the next five seasons, Henry Aaron had his five most productive years as a home run hitter, slugging 203 dingers, leaving him with 713—just one homer short of Babe Ruth's career total—by the end of the 1973 season.

A media whirlwind had descended on Henry Aaron late in the 1973 season that only increased in intensity in early 1974. A black man who played in the recently desegregated South, Aaron was the object of countless death threats as he closed in on one of baseball's most cherished milestones. Nevertheless, Aaron never let anything distract him from playing ball and helping the Braves win games. Although he was well aware of the historical implications of his feat, Aaron displayed the utmost modesty during his time in the limelight. Because of his skill and grace of bearing, Aaron was heralded across the nation as a true American hero.

Henry Aaron retired from Major League Baseball after playing the 1975 and 1976 seasons for the Milwaukee Brewers. Aaron's lifetime batting average was .305. He set a new major league mark with 2,297 RBI, and finished with 755 home runs, making him Major League Baseball's all-time home run king.

CHAPTER THREE

The 500 Club

Mickey Mantle, a switch-hitter, lines an opposite-field home run from the left side of the plate. Like Mays and Aaron, Mantle could do it all and more on the baseball field: he ran like the wind, fielded exceptionally, and hit for power and average. If not for the injuries that shortened his career, Mickey would have joined Willie and Hank at the above-600 home run plateau.

What does it take to become a member of the 500 Club? The first and only requirement is the ability to hit 500 home runs during a major league career. In other words, it takes power and longevity. Some of the game's greatest sluggers failed to reach the 500 plateau. Ralph Kiner hit homers with greater frequency than any player except Babe Ruth, but

Kiner's back debilitated him before he ever hit 400, let alone 500. Some great sluggers, like Hank Greenberg, Johnny Mize, and Joe DiMaggio, lost years to military service; others were felled by injury (like Kiner) or illness (like Lou Gehrig). Then there is the breed of one-dimensional power hitters, like Dave Kingman, Steve Balboni, and

Rob Deer of recent years, who could hit home runs but do little else of value in the batter's box or anywhere else on a baseball field. In contrast, the members of the 500 Club all made huge contributions to the success of their teams over long careers; they were all great players.

JIMMIE FOXX

James Emory "Jimmie" Foxx came to the big leagues from Sudlersville, on the Maryland coast, where he was born in 1907. Foxx was only seventeen years old when the legendary Frank "Home Run" Baker saw the young man play in an Eastern League Game. Still a Philadelphia Athletic at heart, Baker brought the muscular, power-hitting catcher to the attention of Connie Mack. Already blessed with two star catchers, Mack wavered. But Baker was unrelenting: "This boy has as much power as any hitter I've ever seen and that goes for Ruth," declared Baker. Mack heeded Baker's advice and signed Foxx.

By 1928 Foxx was playing as the A's starting first baseman. By 1929 the power surge began, and Foxx was quickly deemed "the right-handed Ruth." The A's won three consecutive pennants from 1929 to 1931 and two World Championships. Foxx clubbed 100 home runs over that span. In the fifth game of the 1930 World Series, with the game scoreless and the Series tied 2-2, Foxx crushed a 2-run home run in the top of the ninth that all but defeated the Cardinals.

Jimmie Foxx was a huge, muscular, agile slugger whose titanic home runs drove fear into the hearts of pitchers. Foxx stood deep in the batter's box, held the bat at the handle, and took a full stride into the pitch. Able to hit to all fields, Foxx had a career .325 average to go with 534 home runs and 1,925 RBI. For the most part, however, Foxx was celebrated for his awesome power. His first-inning home run in the 1935 All-Star Game in Cleveland

was only one Foxx clout of legendary proportion. Once, a Foxx blast reached the Yankee Stadium upper deck where it still had sufficient velocity to break a seat. Foxx hit 30 or more home runs each season from 1929 to 1940. He won three MVP awards (in 1932 and 1933 with the A's, and in 1938 with the Red Sox) and a triple crown in 1933.

As daunting as Foxx was at bat, he was kind and generous as a man. Never able to make sound financial investments, Foxx always found a home in and around baseball after retiring in 1945—as a manager, coach, and announcer. Ted Williams, whom Foxx had tutored in the early 1940s, said of "Double XX": "I truly loved Foxxie." Foxx died at age fifty-nine by choking to death at a dinner party.

Above: Jimmie Foxx is greeted by his teammates after homering in the third inning of Game Two of the 1929 World Series. The homer was Foxx's second in two games. Foxx led the A's as they defeated the Cubs in five games to capture the World Championship.
Right: Foxx, playing for the Red Sox late in his career, blasts his 494th career home run on August 16, 1940, at Fenway Park to move past Lou Gehrig into second place on the all-time home run list, behind Babe Ruth.

MEL OTT

Mel Ott came to the New York Giants in late 1925 at the age of sixteen and stayed for the next twenty-three years. During his tenure Ott was the premier slugger in the National League, belting 511 home runs.

Ott was in his first year of semipro ball in his native Louisiana when the owner of his team, Henry Williams—who happened to be friends with the Giants' legendary manager John McGraw—arranged for Ott to try out with the Giants. Ott passed the audition. Because of Ott's unorthodox batting style, McGraw never lent him out to the minor leagues for fear that a batting coach would alter Ott's unique hitting approach. A left-handed hitter, Ott began with his legs far apart; as the pitcher was in his motion, Ott raised his right (front) leg up to knee level, bringing it down (to only inches from where it started) before making contact. With this approach Ott used his compact, muscular body not only to cover the strike zone, but to utilize a pull-hitting style suited to the short right-field fence at New York's Polo Grounds. In his second full season, 1929, at the ripe age of twenty, the "Boy Bomber" hit .328 with 42 home runs and 151 RBI.

When Ott came of age, he could "homer" in any ballpark at any time; such was his power. In his very first World Series at-bat in 1933, versus Washington, he sent a massive 400-foot drive into the Polo Grounds' right-field bleachers. By the fifth

Left: Mel Ott's joining the Giants in his teens coupled with his power hitting earned him the nickname, the "Boy Bomber." This portrait of Ott in his Giants uniform is from April 9, 1927; he was only eighteen years old. Above: Driving in a run, Ott flies out to right field in a home game against the Brooklyn Dodgers on July 6, 1935. Ott's pull-hitting was suited to the Giants' home at the Polo Grounds, which had a short right-field fence. If Ott's fly was deep enough to drive in a runner, it couldn't have missed being a home run by much.

game, the Giants were looking to close out the Series on the road, but their lead evaporated and the game was tied 3-3 after nine innings. A comeback victory would swing the Series' momentum to the Senators. With two outs in the top of the tenth, Ott sent a blast to dead center field. The Washington outfielder gave chase and jumped to reach over the wall—more than 400 feet from home plate—only to have the ball skim off his glove for a home run. Ott had won the Series for the Giants.

Baseball was Mel Ott's life, and he approached the game with a commitment and dignity that earned him the respect of his peers and fans. In 1942 Ott was rewarded with the status of player-manager. He had a few more productive years as a hitter, but the Giants were never better than mediocre in his six years as manager. Sadly, Ott died in an automobile collision caused by a drunk driver in 1958.

TED WILLIAMS

There can be no correct answer to the question "Who is the greatest hitter of all time?" Yet fans and scholars of every generation have spent countless hours debating the subject. Among recent baseball historians, who have developed numerous strategies to compare players from different eras, a consensus has emerged that two players contributed more to their teams' offensive play than any others: Babe Ruth and Ted Williams.

Williams grew up in San Diego, California. Coming from a troubled household, Ted spent much of his childhood on the city playgrounds, where he began playing ball at an early age. Naturally right-handed, Williams began hitting from the left side of the plate the very first time he picked up a bat. Ted soon developed an unbridled passion for hitting, and in his teens spent hours practicing every day. In school, Ted would carry a bat to classes and go straight to the sandlots after the final bell. His commitment paid off: by the time he reached high school he was his hometown's leading prospect. In 1936, at the tender age of seventeen, he joined San Diego's new minor league team, which had a working agreement with the Boston Red Sox.

After struggling during his first summer facing professional pitching, Williams tore up the Pacific Coast League in 1937. Though Ted was six-foot-four and weighed only 155 pounds at the

Many people have claimed that Ted Williams was as good at hitting a baseball as is humanly possible. Year after year, Williams provided support for this theory by scorching line drives around the fields of the AL. Pitchers admitted they were at a loss when facing the "Splendid Splinter," and that their strategy amounted to damage control. For his part, Williams attributed his success to his love of hitting, hours of practice, and his mental toughness, which allowed him to focus on his task as a batter.

time—he was all arms and legs—his swing was a thing of beauty that no batting coach would dare tamper with. Not that anyone could tell young Ted what to do—he was as arrogant as he was skilled. Williams reported to Red Sox training camp in the spring of 1938, but he was still too green for the majors; pitchers took advantage of his eagerness and had him swinging at bad pitches. The Red Sox management worried that Williams was too stubborn for conventional instruction, so they hired the great Rogers Hornsby to tutor their young star during a final year in the minors. Hornsby espoused confidence, an approach that appealed to his understudy. Hornsby impressed upon Williams that he must never give credit to a pitcher, no matter how skilled, for retiring him. Outs result from a lack of execution on the hitter's part. A patient batter will "get a good ball to hit" in every at-bat. By 1939 Williams was ripe, and headed for the major leagues.

Ted Williams acknowledged that he only had one goal in life: "To walk down the street and have people say 'There's the greatest hitter who ever lived.'" Over the course of his career with the Boston Red Sox (from 1939 to 1960) Williams not only compiled incomparable offensive statistics (unsurpassed in the annals of the game), but impressed upon his contemporaries that no one could possibly hit a baseball any better than the "Splendid Splinter." Tall and thin, Williams was awkward chasing fly balls or running the bases, and he did not possess a great arm. But in the batter's box he was pure, fluid grace. A pull-hitter with a slight uppercut, Williams made more than just solid contact with a pitch; he hit line drives like bullets and home runs like rockets. Ted did not consider himself a home run hitter; to him round-trippers were just line drives with a higher trajectory.

In his rookie year Williams hit .327 with 31 home runs and 145 RBI. Two years later he became the first player in eleven years to hit over .400, batting .406—a feat unequaled since. Ted won six batting titles, four home run crowns, and two AL triple crowns (in 1942 and 1947). In 1957, at the age of thirty-eight, the Splendid Splinter hit .388. Williams amassed 521 career home runs, even though he missed four full years to military service and played half his games in Fenway Park, with its distant right-field fence. Without these two handicaps, it is quite likely that Williams

would have surpassed Babe Ruth's home run total. Nevertheless, Williams and Ruth are the only two players in major league history to hit better than .340 (Ted hit .344 and the Babe .342 over their respective careers) and blast more than 500 home runs.

MICKEY MANTLE

Mickey Mantle followed Babe Ruth and Joe DiMaggio in a succession of superstar Yankees outfielders that spanned the team's forty-year domination of Major League Baseball. Mantle debuted during DiMaggio's final year, 1951. One superstar retired and another arrived on cue. There was no need to break stride (or even blink). The Bronx Bombers won the third of five consecutive world championships in 1951. They won twelve AL pennants and seven World Series during Mantle's first fourteen seasons.

Unfortunately, baseball fans in the 1950s had grown so accustomed to (and apathetic about) Yankee success that they failed to appreciate Mickey Mantle. Yet Yankees teams of the 1950s and early 1960s had to do more than merely don pinstripes and walk on the field to extend baseball's

Mickey Mantle led the Yankees to twelve AL pennants and seven World Series victories in his first fourteen seasons. Mickey followed Joe DiMaggio, Lou Gehrig, and Babe Ruth in the succession of superstars that anchored the greatest dynasty in the history of American sports, the 1920-to-1964 New York Yankees.

greatest dynasty. They had to construct a lasting juggernaut out of competent journeymen, a handful of stars, and their one superstar. Mickey Mantle was the greatest Yankee of his time; his achievements place him among the best ever to play the game.

Mickey Mantle grew up in northern Oklahoma, where his father worked in the lead mines. Elvin "Mutt" Mantle was a die-hard baseball fan who named his son after his favorite player, Mickey Cochrane, the great catcher for the champion A's of the early 1930s. Mutt wanted his son to have a better life than that of a miner, so he provided him with a first-rate education—in baseball. Mutt and Grandpa Charlie began Mickey's lessons when the youngster was only seven years old. Against ol' southpaw Charlie, Mickey batted from the right side; against his right-handed father, the naturally right-handed child switched to the left side of the plate. Thus was born the greatest switch-hitter ever.

Northern Oklahoma was St. Louis Cardinals country, and both Mutt and Mickey were huge Redbird fans. By the time Mickey was a junior in high school, word of his towering home runs, hit from both sides of the plate, spread throughout the region. Naturally, Cardinals scouts were the first to watch Mickey. They seemed impressed and asked him not to sign with anyone until they contacted him. Mickey agreed to wait. In the meantime he captured the attention of a Yankee scout. Mysteriously, muscular young Mickey never heard again from his beloved Cardinals. When graduation day finally arrived, Mickey signed with the only team to offer him a contract, the New York Yankees.

In 1951 expectations ran high for the six-foot, 200-pound, nineteen-year-old rookie. Yankee fans had read about his monstrous blasts and anticipated another Ruth. However, Mantle struggled at the outset of his rookie year and was demoted to the minors. After two months Mickey earned a return ticket to New York, where he played well. However, his season ended horribly when he shattered his left knee during the World Series. Mantle recovered in time for the 1952 season, but he would never play again without pain.

Through 1955, Mickey established himself as a .300 hitter, a good RBI man, a longball threat (30 home runs per year), and an excellent center fielder. Mantle also gained a reputation for occa-

Mickey Mantle slams a game-winning home run in the ninth inning of Game Three of the 1964 World Series against the St. Louis Cardinals. The home run was Mickey's 16th in World Series competition and it broke Babe Ruth's record for the most home runs hit by one player in the Fall Classic. Mantle hit two more homers against the Cardinals during that Series, his twelfth and last. In spite of Mickey's heroics, the Yankees lost the Series in seven games. Mantle holds the record for career post season homers with 18, Reggie Jackson is second with 16, and Lenny Dykstra is first among active players with 10.

sionally launching gargantuan home runs (for example, the shot he hit at Griffith Stadium in Washington on April 17, 1953, recorded at 565 feet, was the longest home run ever officially measured in the major leagues). Nevertheless, fans still griped that Mantle was no DiMaggio, and certainly no Ruth.

In 1956 the Mick silenced his critics by leading the American League with 52 home runs, 130 RBI, and a .353 average, becoming the first Yankee since Lou Gehrig to win a triple crown. From 1956 through 1962, Mantle sustained a level of excellence comparable to any player in history, averaging more than 40 home runs and 100 RBI while hitting above .315.

In 1963 Mantle suffered a severe foot injury. By 1965 the pain in his legs began to hinder his hitting. Still only thirty-three years old, Mick's career was in rapid decline. Mantle retired before the 1969 season with 536 home runs. In 1962 Mantle became the youngest player ever to hit 400 homers, achieving that milestone at age thirty; Babe Ruth, Willie Mays, and Henry Aaron were all thirty-two when they crushed their 400th career round-trippers. If not for debilitating injuries, Mickey Mantle might have topped the list of baseball's home run kings.

Lou Gehrig

....

Yankees great Lou Gehrig would certainly have earned membership in the 500 Club if not for the tragedy that abruptly ended his career. Gehrig began the 1939 season with 493 home runs and an astounding record of playing in 2,122 consecutive games. However, Gehrig felt increasingly weak during the season's first eight games, and on May 2, 1939, he benched himself. Later in the month, Gehrig was diagnosed with a rare degenerative nerve disorder, amyotrophic lateral sclerosis (now known as Lou Gehrig's disease), and was told he had only a slight chance of survival. On July 4, 1939, the Yankees held Lou Gehrig Day in honor of their fallen hero. In one of baseball's most moving and poetic moments, Gehrig told a packed house that "today, I consider myself the luckiest man on the face of the earth." Gehrig's body may have betrayed him, but his spirit was stronger than ever. Gehrig finished his career with 493 home runs, 1990 RBI, and a .340 batting average. The "Iron Man" holds the record for most consecutive games played (which is currently being challenged by Cal Ripken, Jr.), and he also hit more grand slams, 23, than anyone else in baseball history. Gehrig still holds the AL RBI record with the 184 runs he batted in during 1931. He won the AL triple crown in 1934. Overall he won five RBI titles, three home run crowns, and batted over .300 for twelve straight seasons. Lou Gehrig died at the age of thirty-seven on June 2, 1941.

Lou Gehrig is pictured here on the steps of the Yankees dugout in Detroit on May 2, 1939, the fateful day when the Iron Horse could play no longer. He pulled himself from the starting lineup and ended his streak of consecutive games played at 2,130. Within a few weeks Gehrig's ailment was diagnosed as a deadly disease.

EDDIE MATHEWS

Eddie Mathews was the power-hitting third baseman for the great Milwaukee Braves teams of the late 1950s. Eddie was born in north Texas, and his family moved to California during his childhood. When Mathews was inducted into the Hall of Fame he recalled the evening baseball lessons his parents gave him: "My mother used to pitch to me and my father would shag balls. If I hit one up the middle, close to my mother, I'd have some extra chores to do. My mother was instrumental in making me a pull-hitter." Eddie was the star of Santa Monica High School, and the Braves signed him after graduation in 1949.

Mathews, who hit left-handed and threw right-handed, progressed rapidly through the minor league ranks. The Braves were rebuilding and were willing to experiment with young talent, so in 1952 the twenty-year-old Eddie Mathews became an everyday starter for the Boston Braves.

Mathews responded well to the challenge, breaking two rookie records by smashing 25 home runs in the season and hitting 3 home runs in one game. Mathews still needed to improve: he led the National League in strikeouts with 115.

In 1953 the Braves moved to Milwaukee and everything changed. "I don't think any city has ever gone as crazy over a baseball team as the city of Milwaukee did when the Braves arrived there in 1953," observed Mathews some thirty-five years later. No doubt inspired by the fans' enthusiasm, the young Braves began to click, and behind strong, veteran pitching stayed in contention until September. Mathews was particularly impressive, leading the National League with 47 homers while driving in 135 RBI and batting .302. Mathews was only twenty-one years old.

From 1953 to 1960 Mathews averaged nearly 40 home runs (he earned a second home run title in 1959), more than 100 RBI, and batted consistently above .280. In 1954 the Braves added a

Third baseman Eddie Mathews of the Milwaukee Braves was young, clean-cut, handsome, well-spoken, and could hit the ball into the next county—or at least out of County Stadium. Mathews, Henry Aaron, and Joe Adcock formed a "murderers' row" on the great Braves teams of the late 1950s.

rookie right fielder named Henry Aaron to their everyday lineup. Mathews and Aaron provided the power core for a team that captured back-to-back pennants in 1957 and 1958. In the 1957 October Classic Mathews hit a home run in the bottom of the tenth inning of Game Four to tie the Series 2-2. The Braves went on to defeat the Yankees in seven games, sending baseball-crazed Milwaukee into pandemonium. The Yankees, however, rebounded to defeat the Braves in seven games in 1958.

Mathews and Aaron remained with the Braves in the early 1960s as the great team deteriorated. The Milwaukee fans, however, abandoned the Braves, convinced that the club's ownership was not committed to maintaining a winning tradition. By 1966 Mathews and Aaron were playing their last season together for the Atlanta Braves. The pair hit more home runs, 863, than any two teammates in history. Mathews compiled 512 home runs during a career that ended with the 1968 world champion Detroit Tigers. Eddie Mathews managed the Braves in the early 1970s and, thus, was Hank Aaron's skipper on the night he broke Babe Ruth's all-time home run record.

Eddie Mathews takes off for first base while following the flight of a ball he has just hit towards the right field bleachers at Milwaukee's County Stadium. Mathews and Henry Aaron hit more home runs during their many years together on the Braves than any pair of teammates in major league history.

ERNIE BANKS

Ernie Banks was arguably the greatest player in Chicago Cubs history. For nineteen seasons, Banks started as shortstop or first baseman for the northsiders, and holds virtually every lifetime batting record for the club. Yet it was Banks' cheerful disposition that made him the most popular player in Chicago history and earned him the nickname "Mr. Cub."

Banks was raised in Dallas, Texas, where he excelled at baseball, basketball, and football in high school. Banks joined the Amarillo Colts, an all-black semipro team, after the Colts' manager saw Banks play at a YMCA softball game. In 1950, at the age of nineteen, Banks was signed by the Kansas City Monarchs of the Negro Leagues. However, Ernie was drafted into the U.S. Army and spent the 1951 and 1952 seasons overseas. When he returned to the United States, Banks chose to return to the Monarchs rather than play minor league ball in the Indians or Dodgers organizations. In September 1953 the Cubs decided Banks was worth the gamble and purchased his contract from the Monarchs. Ernie never played a day in the minors. In fact, the young, sleek shortstop played in a record 424 consecutive games at the start of his major league career.

At six-foot-one and 180 pounds, Banks was slim, but his exceptionally strong wrists provided him with unexpected power. In 1955 he set a record with five grand slams in one season. Ernie amazed Cubs fans as he seemed to improve every year. In 1958 Banks led the National League with 47 home runs, and added 129 RBI while hitting .313 to become the first player ever to be named league MVP on a losing team. In 1959 Banks crushed 45 home runs, drove in 143 runs (the most in the senior circuit in twenty-two years), hit .303, and broke the all-time record for fielding percentage by a shortstop (.985). On another losing team, Ernie became the first player ever to win back-to-back MVP awards. Banks must have made an incredible impression on his contemporaries to break such a long-standing precedent and gain recognition as the best player in the National League for two years in a row.

Over Banks' long career with the team, the Cubs only contended once for the pennant. Nevertheless, Ernie came to the ballpark every day full of joy at the prospect of playing baseball.

Ernie Banks practices before a game. Widely regarded as the greatest player never to appear in a World Series, "Mr. Cub" was an excellent fielding shortstop and a tremendous hitter. However, his unique place in Chicago baseball lore as the most loved player in the history of the city stems as much from his enthusiasm for the game (which never waned even though the Cubs were perennial also-rans) as it does from his superb playing.

Banks never let his adoring fans down, spending hours signing autographs and talking with kids. Banks' 500th home run on May 12, 1970, in Chicago's Wrigley Field was one of the most celebrated moments in Cubs history. Banks retired after the 1971 season with 512 career home runs.

HARMON KILLEBREW

By late spring 1954, young Harmon Killebrew was a legend in western Idaho. The son of a sheriff, Harmon starred in basketball, football, and baseball for Payette High School. After his senior year he began ripping up the local semipro league like no one had before him. Unfortunately, western Idaho was off the beaten path for major league scouts. Killebrew was planning to drop his bat and glove at the end of the summer and attend a small local liberal arts college. However, Idaho Senator Herman Welker got word of Killebrew's exploits and urged Washington Senators owner Clark Griffith to send someone to watch him. On June 19, 1954, the Senators signed Killebrew to a bonus contract. At the time he was batting .847.

Bonus players had to remain with the major league club for two seasons, and Killebrew played sparingly in 1954 (13 at-bats) and 1955 (80 at-bats). He spent the balance of the following three seasons in the minors, and had his proper debut with the Senators in 1959. In the first month of the season, Killebrew raised some eyebrows by slugging 8 homers in one twelve-game stretch. He led the majors with 28 home runs at midseason, but cooled down to tie for the league lead with 42.

A six-foot-tall 190-pounder, the "Killer" moved with Griffith's franchise to Minnesota in 1961. He led the American League in home runs every year from 1962 through 1964 with 48, 45, and 49, respectively. A powerful right-handed batter, Killebrew had no set defensive position throughout his career; he played third base, outfield, and first base, and was eventually a designated hitter. Killebrew won a total of six AL home run titles, one of them in 1969, when he hit 49 round-trippers, knocked in 140 runs, and batted .276 while walking 145 times to earn the league's MVP award. Immensely popular in Minnesota, the soft-spoken slugger led the Twins to the AL pennant in 1965 and AL West titles in 1969 and 1970. In 8,147 career at-bats, Killebrew was never asked to bunt, a major league record. He hit 573 career home runs, placing him fifth on the all-time list.

Above: Harmon Killebrew was a gentle, soft-spoken man whose nickname was "Killer" because on a baseball field he was known for one thing: hitting the living daylights out of a ball. Killebrew's total of 573 career home runs is the fifth-highest of all time. Left: Killebrew displays his mighty swing as he smashes a double for the Minnesota Twins in May of 1962. Harmon's intimidating presence was the centerpiece of the Twins offense on teams that captured one pennant (1965) and two divisional crowns (1969 and 1970).

Frank Robinson had one of the most remarkable careers in the history of baseball. He began as a celebrated star in little league and never let up. He was NL Rookie of the Year in 1956 with the Reds and won the NL MVP in 1961 and the AL MVP in 1966 to become the only player ever to win the award in both leagues. Robinson was the primary star on five pennant-winning teams and two Baltimore Orioles world championship teams (1966 and 1970). In 1975 he became the first African-American manager in major league history, with the Cleveland Indians. He retired with 586 career home runs, the fourth-highest total ever.

FRANK ROBINSON

Frank Robinson was a tall, thin, yet powerful out-fielder—in the mold of Ted Williams and Joe DiMaggio—who terrorized major league pitching from 1956 until the mid-1970s. Robinson grew up in Oakland, California, where he led his American Legion team to two consecutive national titles in 1949 and 1950. Drafted after high school by the Cincinnati Reds in 1953, Robinson spent three years in the minors before beginning the 1956 campaign with the Reds. Frank had a great first year, tying the freshman record for homers with 38, leading the league in runs scored with 122, hitting .290, and winning the NL Rookie of the Year Award. A fierce competitor, the six-foot-one, 194-pound Robinson became the focal point of the Reds offense. In his ten years with the club, Robinson averaged over 30 home runs and 100 RBI per year, while batting over .300. His two best seasons were 1961 and 1962, when his stats were 37 home runs, 124 RBI, and a .325 average, and 39 home runs, 136 RBI, and a .342 percentage, respectively. He won the NL MVP in 1961, when the upstart Reds won the pennant.

Following the 1965 season the Reds shocked the baseball world by trading their star outfielder to the Baltimore Orioles. Robinson responded by having his greatest season, hitting .316, driving in 122 runs, and smashing 49 home runs, all of which earned him the AL triple crown. The Orioles won the pennant and then swept the Dodgers in four games to capture the franchise's first World Series championship. When Robinson won the 1966 AL MVP, he became the only player ever to win the award in both major leagues. The Robinson-led Orioles suffered through two injury-plagued seasons and then won three consecutive pennants (1969 to 1971) and the 1970 World Series.

An intelligent, insightful man, Robinson had announced his desire to manage in his 1968 book, *My Life is Baseball*. In 1975 the Cleveland Indians appointed Robinson player-manager, making him the major leagues' first African-American manager. Robinson retired as a player in 1976 with a career .294 average and 586 home runs, the fourth-highest home run total in baseball history. He has managed the Indians, Giants, and Orioles. He won the NL Manager of the Year Award in 1982 for guiding an underdog Giants team to within two games of the NL West crown.

WILLIE McCOVEY

Willie McCovey was a fearsome hitter. He stood six-foot-four and weighed 198 pounds, batted and threw left, and belted rockets into right field with his bat. In a career that spanned from 1959 to 1980, "Stretch" smashed 521 home runs.

McCovey joined the Giants with a bang in 1959, winning Rookie of the Year honors by hitting .354 with 13 home runs and 38 RBI in only 192 at-bats. However, the Giants were so overloaded with talent in the early 1960s that McCovey had no place to play on a regular basis. Orlando Cepeda was an established (and awesome) star at first base, and McCovey's weak outfield play made the Giants wary of trading any of the three highly skilled Alou brothers. Still, the Giants adamantly refused to trade a talent like McCovey, so he became the greatest player ever to spend his first five seasons as a spot-starter and pinch-hitter extraordinaire.

It was in this capacity that McCovey participated in the 1962 World Series. Down 1-0 against the Yankees in the bottom of the ninth of the seventh game, with two outs and a runner on first, McCovey watched from the on-deck circle as Willie Mays doubled to right field. Roger Maris fielded the ball perfectly, and his strong throw held Matty Alou at third base. McCovey stepped to the plate against Ralph Terry (who had surrendered a two-run homer to McCovey in Game Two to give the Giants a 2-0 victory). With Cepeda on deck, the Yankees decided to pitch to McCovey. On Terry's first pitch McCovey scorched a line drive to right field, but second baseman Bobby Richardson timed a perfect leap and caught the ball to end the game and win the World Series for the Yankees. McCovey had gone from hero to heartbreaker in an instant.

It wasn't until 1965, when Cepeda was injured and then subsequently traded, that McCovey established himself as the Giants' everyday first baseman. From 1965 through 1970, Willie's offensive production was awesome, averaging 38 home runs and 106 RBI a year. His peak season was 1969, when he won his second consecutive home run crown (his third overall) with 45 home runs, had 126 RBI, hit .320, and won the NL MVP.

A soft-spoken—even shy—man from Mobile, Alabama, Willie McCovey was probably the most

Willie "Stretch" McCovey of the San Francisco Giants reaches out and sends the ball searing towards the bleachers. McCovey was a great hitter who had one of the strangest beginnings to a major league career. Willie won the NL Rookie of the Year in 1959, but the Giants were so laden with talent that McCovey did not start regularly for a few years. Had "Stretch" been able to play more in his early years with the Giants, he would have added greatly to his career home run total.

beloved player in San Francisco Giants history. McCovey played for the Giants until 1973, and then was traded to San Diego. Attendance at Giants games consequently plummeted. McCovey's production fell off. In 1976 McCovey was traded to Oakland, but he refused to play. The Giants contacted Willie in the off-season, and come springtime "Big Mac" was back in Giants black-and-orange. In 1977 Willie sparked a Giants renaissance with his best season since 1973, and the fans flooded back to Candlestick Park. McCovey retired in 1980 and joined the Giants' front office.

REGGIE JACKSON

Reggie Jackson was baseball's most dynamic superstar in the 1970s; if anyone said otherwise, Jackson was quick to correct them. Cocky and irreverent, Jackson took a page from Muhammad Ali's book of braggadocio. Traditionalists and managers complained about Jackson's boasting and lackadaisical defensive play, but just about every year in the post season, "Mr. October" silenced his critics. Jackson's teams won eleven divisional titles, six pennants, and five World Series—numbers unrivaled in the years since the Yankee dynasty.

Reggie Jackson grew up in suburban Philadelphia, and excelled at four sports in high school. He received a football scholarship from Arizona State University, but quit the team when coach Frank Kush switched him from tight end to cornerback—Jackson refused to play only defense. So Reggie tried out for the baseball team. Soon he was receiving national attention for his massive home run blasts. In 1966, his senior season, Reggie was named the college player of the year. The A's selected Jackson second in the draft, after the Mets bypassed him in favor of a catcher who wound up never playing in the majors.

A six-foot, 206-pounder who batted and threw left-handed, Jackson debuted with the Kansas City A's in 1967, and followed the franchise to Oakland in 1968. The following season Jackson captured the major league spotlight by hitting 29 home runs by the end of June, which put him ahead of Maris' 1961 pace and on a pace to hit 67 for the season. He was red hot with 45 coming into September, but cooled off to finish with only 47 (third in the American League that year). At the 1971 All-Star Game, Reggie won headlines again by smashing a ball onto the roof of Tiger Stadium for a home run. When the A's won three consecutive World Series (1972 to 1974), Jackson was their primary offensive weapon. He won both the AL and World Series MVP awards in 1973. Jackson was traded to Baltimore in 1976, and when his contract expired at the end of the season he became the most celebrated free agent to date. Jackson signed with the Yankees, and throughout the 1977 season he was the centerpiece of a Bronx soap opera involving Yankees owner George Steinbrenner, manager Billy Martin, and other star players. By the time of his phenomenal 5-home-run World Series, "Reggie" was a household name.

In the batter's box Reggie stood slightly hunched, his powerful muscles ready to uncoil, and glared at the pitchers from behind his tinted glasses. When the pitch came, Reggie took a full stride and unleashed a mighty swing. If he missed, the crowd would gasp; when he made clean contact, the product was potent and graceful. In a career that spanned twenty-one seasons, Jackson hit 563 home runs, the sixth-highest total ever.

Above: The inimitable Reggie Jackson ranks sixth on the all-time list with 563 career home runs. Right: Jackson connects for a mammoth home run in the 1978 AL East playoff against the Red Sox. As always, Reggie completes his home run swing poised to appreciate the flight of the ball.

MIKE SCHMIDT

Mike Schmidt was drafted by the Phillies from Ohio University in 1971 in the second round. The power-hitting third baseman spent two full years in the minors and struggled on an inexperienced Phillies team in his first full year. However, in 1974 Schmidt had a superb year—36 home runs, 116 RBI, and a .282 average—and established himself, along with ace pitcher Steve Carlton, as one of the cornerstones around which the Phillies would construct a championship-caliber team. By 1980 that team had won four of five NL East titles and the 1980 NL pennant and World Series Championship. Over these years, Schmidt established himself as the premier power hitter in the National League, averaging an incredible 38 home runs and 107 RBI per season.

A closer analysis of Mike Schmidt's statistics reveals the depth of his contribution to the team. Schmidt was a disciplined power hitter who, though he often struck out, took a tremendous number of walks. Thus, Schmidt was on base much more than his career .267 batting average would suggest, a fact attested to by the huge number of runs he scored each year (an average of 105). When Schmidt did hit, he hit for power. This lethal combination of high slugging and on-base percentages is unparalleled among his generation. Combine these offensive attributes with Schmidt's eleven Gold Gloves and it is understandable why Schmidt was hailed not only as one of the two best all-around players of his time (along with Joe Morgan), but also as one of the greatest third baseman of all time.

At his peak from 1980 to 1983, Schmidt and pitcher Steve Carlton carried a team of over-the-hill stars and quality journeymen to major league transcendence—an astounding accomplishment in the highly competitive (post-expansion and free-agency) years in which Schmidt flourished. Schmidt won the NL and World Series MVP awards in 1980, a year in which he slugged 48 home runs, knocked in 121 runs, and batted .286. Schmidt maintained his excellence throughout the 1980s, winning the NL MVP award again in 1981 and a third time in 1986. A proud competitor, he retired abruptly in 1989 at the age of thirty-eight when he sensed he could not fully recover from an injury sustained in late 1988. With 548 home runs, Schmidt placed seventh on the all-time list. A hard worker without a lot of flash, Schmidt did not covet the cult of personality afforded superstars; he only made headlines with his bat and glove.

Mike Schmidt gazes up at a pop fly down the first baseline, hoping the ball reaches the stands. Schmidt generated such tremendous bat speed that even his pop-ups were a sight to behold. Schmidt's 548 career home runs places him seventh on the all-time list.

Military hero Hank Greenberg plays ball with the Detroit Tigers.

Legendary St. Louis Cardinal Stan Musial.

Handicapped Sluggers: Long Fences and Military Duty

A classic photograph of Joltin' Joe's classic follow-through.

Ted Williams blasts a line drive towards the bleachers.

World War II interrupted the careers of almost an entire generation of players, severely reducing the career home run totals of sluggers like Joe DiMaggio, Hank Greenberg, and Ted Williams.

Joltin' Joe DiMaggio was certainly one of the greatest baseball players ever; he led the Yankees to nine World Series titles in the thirteen full seasons he played from 1936 to 1951. However, Joe suffered a triple whammy when it came to his career home run total: he missed three prime years to military service; he played in a home stadium not conducive to right-handed power hitters; and he was forced into retirement by a chronic back injury. Without these three handicaps, Joe's home run total of 361 would no doubt have been higher.

Hammerin' Hank Greenberg, who hit 331 career home runs, sacrificed four full seasons to World War II (at the time Hank was averaging 40 home runs per year) and one more because of an injury; he also retired early. Ted Williams slugged 521 home runs even though he missed four full years to military service (three to World War II and one to the Korean War), and played in a stadium that had a distant right-field fence that lessened Williams' seasonal home run totals. Just before the outbreak of World War II, Yankees and Red Sox management entertained the idea of a DiMaggio-for-Williams swap that would have rectified their respective sluggers' predicaments with their home fields. However, both front offices came to their senses, realizing that the risk involved in such a trade was too great.

Stan Musial was the greatest hitter in the major leagues during the World War II years. An eighteen-year-old rookie in 1941, Musial was so young that he only missed one season, 1945, to military service. A true legend at the plate, Musial remained the premier batter in the senior circuit throughout the 1940s and 1950s. More noted for line drives than the longball, "Stan the Man" did hit 475 round-trippers during his twenty-three-year career, an average of just over 20 per season. However, Musial banged out so many doubles and triples that he ranks ninth in career slugging percentage (.559). Since he was averaging only 10 to 15 home runs per year as a youngster in the mid-forties, it seems unlikely that his one-year hiatus kept him from the 500 Club.

The 50-Plus Club

The record for the most home runs in one year is the most cherished single-season mark in all of baseball. New pennant champions are crowned each autumn, but serious assaults on the 60-home-run plateau are a rarity. If a player approaches the end of the season with a legitimate shot at the record, it doesn't matter if his team is in last place, he becomes the center of a media whirlwind. The pressure is intense: all eyes are on him and pitchers try a little harder to retire him.

Since the days of Babe Ruth only one player, Roger Maris, surmounted all the obstacles to reach 60. In 1961 Maris blasted 61 home runs to break Ruth's mark of 60, set in 1927. However, since the 1961 schedule called for eight more games than were played in 1927, then-commissioner Ford Frick decreed that if Maris did not equal Ruth's record by the 154th game the Yankees played in 1961, a new record established in the final eight games of the season would enter the record books with an asterisk beside it, denoting Maris' scheduling advantage. Thus, officially there remain two records, though Maris' 61 has become accepted as the standard.

The magnitude of Maris' and Ruth's accomplishments is reflected by the fact that only twelve players have ever hit 50 homers in a season. Of the fourteen players who surpassed 500 career home runs, ten never reached the milestone season of 50 (including Henry Aaron). Five players slammed 50 home runs more than once: Jimmie Foxx, Ralph Kiner, Mickey Mantle, and Willie Mays all did it twice; the incomparable Babe Ruth managed the feat four times. The other seven 50-plus hitters are Hank Greenberg, Hack Wilson, George Foster, Johnny Mize, Cecil Fielder, Albert Belle, and, of course, Roger Maris.

The one and only Babe heads down to first watching the flight of the ball he just launched. Only twelve players have ever hit 50 or more home runs in a season, and the feat itself has only been done eighteen times. The Babe passed the milestone four times, while Jimmie Foxx, Ralph Kiner, Mickey Mantle, and Willie Mays each did so twice.

ROGER MARIS: 61 IN '61

The 1961 season is synonymous in baseball with the accomplishments of one man: Roger Maris. Entering the season, expectations were running high for Maris, the 1960 AL MVP, but no one expected what happened. Maris, who had never hit more than 39 home runs in a season, and teammate Mickey Mantle—the M&M boys—went on a season-long assault on Babe Ruth's single-season record of 60 home runs. In the end, Maris not only outdueled the Mick but surpassed the Babe.

Unlike Mantle, Maris was not a career-long Yankees superstar. The North Dakota native—who batted left-handed, threw right-handed, and played right field—came through the Cleveland Indians farm system. After debuting with the Indians in 1957, Maris was traded to the Kansas City Athletics in mid-1958. After contributing 16 homers and a .273 average to the A's effort in 1959, Maris was traded to the Yankees. All of a sudden Maris caught fire, belting 39 home runs,

hitting .283, and leading the American League with 112 RBI in 1960.

Maris struggled at the outset of the 1961 season, hitting around .200 with only 4 home runs after five weeks of play. Yankee President Dan Topping pulled Maris aside and gave him this advice: "Don't worry about your batting average. Shoot for the fences. It won't cost you in your contract. We'll pay you on the basis of home runs and RBI." The assault began. On May 30 Maris hit his 10th home run. Number 20 came only twelve days later; his 30th was hit on July 2, and his 40th on July 25.

As Maris' home run total grew, so did the pressure. Maris did not respond well to the attention. Mantle, a veteran of the media saturation annually bestowed upon the dynastic Yankees, had learned how to deal with the press and tried to counsel Maris. Nevertheless, the media found Maris "sullen," "arrogant," and "surly." Furthermore, Yankees fans clearly were rooting for Mantle over the upstart Maris, and the

Above: The M&M boys pose in the Yankees locker room following a 7-6 victory over the Senators on July 1, 1961. In the game, Mantle blasted his 26th and 27th home runs of the season, tying Maris for the league lead, until Roger hit his 28th with one man on in the bottom of the ninth to end the game.
Left: Roger Maris of the New York Yankees begins to leave home plate after belting his record-setting 61st round-tripper of the year on the last day of the 1961 season.

The 49ers

....

The large number of players who have stalled at 49 home runs in a season provides ample evidence of the pressure players feel as they strive for established goals. While Jimmie Foxx (a slugger who finished six seasons with 48 home runs) was the only player to hit exactly 50 home runs, in 1938 there are ten 49ers in the record books for that year. Babe Ruth was the first to fall one short of the milestone, in 1930. Lou Gehrig accomplished the feat twice, in 1934 and 1936. Cincinnati slugger Ted Kluszewski fell one short in 1959, as did Willie Mays in 1962. Harmon Killebrew equaled Gehrig's efforts with 49 in 1964 and 1969. Frank Robinson posted a 49 in 1966. In 1987 the A's Mark McGuire set the rookie record by hitting 49, and Andre Dawson of the Cubs matched his total that year. The abundance of talented sluggers who stop at 49 homers in a season is clearly not a statistical anamoly—it is a psychological phenomenon.

Of the ten 49ers, only Lou Gehrig in 1934 connected for his final home run on the last day of the regular season. Willie Mays belted numbers 48 and 49 in the first game of a playoff with the Dodgers in 1962, and then failed to launch one in the final two games of the mini-series. Ruth in 1930, Killebrew in 1969, and Dawson in 1987 all knocked number 49 out of the park in the penultimate game of their respective seasons. Killebrew had two complete games to try to hit number 50 in 1964, but failed. Gehrig had three games remaining in 1936 after he reached 49. By failing to homer in his last five games of 1987, Mark McGwire fell 1 home run short of becoming the first rookie ever to hit 50. However, the prize for "most frustrated slugger" goes to two players: Frank Robinson (in 1966) and Ted Kluszewski (in 1954), who both failed to hit a home run in the final eight games of their almost-milestone seasons.

Lou Gehrig is pictured here alongside Babe Ruth during the 1935 season, when Ruth finished his career with the Boston Braves. Eight years earlier Gehrig and Ruth had been teammates on the legendary 1927 Yankees. The two sluggers provided all the drama in the AL that year as they both chased Ruth's 1921 home run record. Thanks to a torrid final month, the Bambino set a new mark on the final day of the 1927 season. Below: Oakland A's slugger Mark McGwire.

right fielder resented this. The tension grew along with Maris' home run total. As the season neared its end, Maris' green eyes were surrounded by dark circles, he never smiled, and his hair started falling out in tufts. Later he would describe the season as "misery," though his home run swing did not abandon him.

On August 31 Maris' home run total was 51 and Mantle's was 48. By the end of a Yankees home stand on September 10, Maris' twenty-sixth birthday, Maris had 56 homers, Mantle had 53, and the Yankees had virtually secured the pennant. Then Mantle came down with the flu and hit only one more home run the rest of the season. Maris hit a slump and didn't homer again until September 16. He hit another round-tripper the next day, and when he spoke to the press he was so exhausted he was barely able to whisper. Everywhere Maris went the press and fans mobbed him; he lived under a constant barrage of the same questions: "Will you break the record?" "Will you beat out Mantle?" "Will you hit a home run today?"

Maris had played 151 games and hit 58 home runs—only the immortal Sultan of Swat had ever smashed more homers in a season. Maris had eleven games left, but only three more if he wanted to avoid the asterisk. After he failed to homer during a doubleheader on September 19, he entered his 154th game needing two home runs to tie Ruth. Unfortunately a stiff wind was blowing in from right field at Baltimore's Memorial Stadium. In the first inning the wind turned a sure home run into an out. Maris succeeded in homering in the fourth inning, but the wind turned another home run blast into a deep out in the seventh inning. In the ninth Maris grounded back to ace reliever and knuckleballer Hoyt Wilhelm for the final out of a rare Yankees defeat.

Maris begrudgingly accepted the commissioner's decree about the asterisk. Just the same, Maris failed to homer for four games, and noted: "I thought the pressure would be off me after the 154th game, but I was wrong. It's worse than ever now. The way this is going, I've got five games left, and I don't think I'll hit 60 by the end of the season." But in the fourth to last game of the year, in the third inning with two out and the bases empty, Maris sent number 60, a two-ball, two-strike pitch, into the right-field third deck at Yankee Stadium. In the final weekend of the season the Red Sox came to the Bronx. Maris did not homer in the first and second games, so it came down to the final day. When Maris broke a scoreless tie with a solo shot in the third, Maris' legend was secured: 61 in '61.

Maris' offensive production fell back to earth in 1962: he hit 33 home runs and drove in 100 runs (compared to 142 in '61), and his batting average dropped to .256 from the .269 mark of his second MVP year. The Yankees captured the AL pennant during his first five years and then collapsed all the way to last place by 1966. Maris was traded to St. Louis in 1967 and became an integral part of the Cardinals' World Championship team that year. He retired following the 1968 season—

after another Cardinal pennant—having compiled 275 home runs across his twelve-year career. Maris died of cancer in 1985; he was only fifty years old.

Tony Kubek, the Yankees' starting shortstop in 1961, summarized Roger Maris' legendary accomplishment:

That year, Roger had supreme confidence in himself. It was as if he were saying, "The only person who can beat me is me." He refused to be distracted and turned all that pressure in one direction—beating the record. Being in New York, the media capital of the world, brought out the best in Roger that sea-

son. The more obstacles placed in front of him, the better he played. That is why Roger's feeling of relief was followed almost immediately by one of vindication. He had defeated everyone who was pulling against him and showed his strength at the same time.

BABE RUTH: 60 IN '27

From 1922 through 1926, Babe Ruth led the major leagues in home runs and slugging percentage three times, and even led the AL in batting in 1924. Ruth was still the most feared slugger in the game, yet his days of effortlessly outdoing himself each season seemed over. Then came 1927.

The one and only Bambino smiles, surrounded by his most cherished fans. When Ruth (who had been put in an orphanage by his parents) traveled the country, he always found time to spend with the children, who universally adored him. While dignitaries and celebrities were usually offered a perfunctory handshake, Ruth seemed to have plenty of time for the children he met.

All season long the defending AL champion Yankees outclassed the field of the junior circuit. The only real drama surrounding the club was whether Ruth or young slugger Lou Gehrig could break the Babe's record of 59 home runs. On August 10, the twenty-four-year-old first baseman led the legend, 38 to 35. But once Gehrig, who was hitting behind Ruth, was established as a threat, hurlers could no longer pitch around the Bambino. Consequently, Ruth was seeing hittable pitches for the first time in years. The Babe's late-season production was spectacular; he crushed 25 homers in 42 games after August 10. Gehrig managed only 9 round-trippers the rest of the way. Their combined season total of 107 home runs remains the second-highest ever, after the M&M boys of 1961.

With five games remaining Ruth was three short of the record, and pitchers had returned to being cautious with the red-hot Babe. The nation's eyes were focused on their hero and there was no way he'd let 'em down. Ruth homered each day through the second-to-last game of the season to become the first player ever to reach the 60 plateau. At the age of thirty-two Ruth let his minions know he was still king.

BABE RUTH: 59 IN '21

It was the year after the Black Sox scandal broke and a year after Babe Ruth had begun to revolutionize the way the game was played. It was the year fans and owners alike looked to the twenty-

six-year-old slugger to continue his awesome display of power, to take everyone's mind off the game's seamy underside. It was the year the Sultan of Swat established himself as more than a one-year fluke and led the Yankees to their first pennant ever. It was 1921, the year that Babe Ruth had one of the greatest seasons ever by a batter.

Ruth not only hit a record 59 home runs, but set a new record with 171 RBI (his highest total). Ruth fell one thousandth of a point shy of his still-standing record for the highest slugging percentage, .847, established the previous year. Ruth batted .378 and walked so frequently (144 times) that his on-base percentage was above .500. By 1921 pitchers knew all too well the havoc wrought by Ruth, but found no way to avoid it. By the end of the year, Ruth was no longer a novelty—he was the United States' greatest hero.

JIMMIE FOXX: 58 IN '32

The years 1929, 1930, and 1931 were Jimmie Foxx's first three as a starter for Connie Mack's Philadelphia A's. Not coincidentally, the A's won the AL pennant each of the three years and won the World Series in 1929 and 1930. Over those three seasons "Double XX" crushed exactly 100 home runs (30, 37, and 33, respectively), some of which were of mammoth proportions. Jimmie Foxx, not yet twenty-four years of age, was just coming into his own.

In 1932, as the A's fell to a distant second behind the Yankees, Foxx made an all-out assault

Above: Twenty-three-year-old Jimmie Foxx is seen here shortly before the 1931 World Series. The A's won the Series in 1929 and 1930, but were derailed by the St. Louis Cardinal Gas-House Gang in 1931. Connie Mack began to dismantle the A's dynasty following the loss to St. Louis, but the young Foxx, who was just coming into his own, later challenged Ruth's single-season home run record in 1932 and won the triple crown in 1933.

Opposite page, top left, to above, right: This sequence of photos was taken while Hank Greenberg was practicing in the batting cages at Yankee Stadium before a game in 1938. Notice how Greenberg, a tall and strong man, took advantage of his size by fully extending his arms when swinging, a technique that generates great power.

on Babe Ruth's record of 60 home runs. With twenty-two days left in the season, Foxx, with 51 homers, was well ahead of Ruth's pace, but suffered a wrist injury falling off a stepladder at his home. He only connected for 2 more homers over the next seventeen days. Foxx finished the season with a flurry, hitting 5 home runs in five days—including 1 in 3 at-bats on the final day of the season—for a total of 58. Actually, Foxx did hit 2 other home runs that season, but they came during the first five innings of games that were canceled because of rain, thus disallowing the home runs. Nevertheless, Foxx had a spectacular season, winning the league MVP award, batting .364 with 169 RBI, and smashing 58 home runs. He missed the triple crown by three percentage points, but Foxx captured that honor the next year, though with lower numbers: 48 home runs, 163 RBI, and a .356 average.

HANK GREENBERG: 58 IN '38

Hank Greenberg hit his 58th home run with five games remaining in the 1938 season. Three more blasts and Hammerin' Hank, the Detroit Tigers' six-foot-four first baseman, would surpass the Babe. National attention focused on Greenberg's assault on the 60 mark and on his heritage.

Henry Benjamin Greenberg was not the first Jewish player in the major leagues, but he was the first Jewish superstar. In 1938 anti-Semitism was a very real and virulent threat to Jews in the United States: Father Coughlin preached a gospel of Jewish hate on the radio, while in Europe the Nazis were building history's greatest war machine with the intention of destroying the international Jewish population. Against this backdrop, Hank Greenberg assumed the national spotlight. Understandably, Jews looked to Greenberg in much the same way blacks looked to Jackie Robinson in 1947: they hoped that their hero could educate a nation by performing with brilliance and discipline, thus dispelling widespread racial stereotypes. Greenberg, like Robinson, did just that.

By 1938 Greenberg was well established as a star. The son of Romanian immigrants, Greenberg was born on January 1, 1911 (1-1-11), in Manhattan's Greenwich Village. His family moved to the Bronx when he was six. Hank always loved baseball and practiced obsessively. A four-sport star in high school, Greenberg rejected the Yankees' offer because he knew Lou Gehrig would start at first base, and signed instead with the Detroit Tigers. Greenberg was the Tigers' starting first baseman by 1933 and an established star by 1934. Over his career, Greenberg led the Tigers to four pennants, in 1934, 1935, 1940, and 1945, and to two World Series titles, in 1935 and 1945. This number of pennants is all the more incredible considering that Greenberg served in the armed forces from 1941 to 1944 and that the Gehrig/DiMaggio Yankees dynasty ruled the

Above: Hank Greenberg was the cornerstone of the great Tigers teams of the 1930s and 1940s, leading Detroit to pennants in 1934, 1935, 1940, and 1945. The Tigers run of pennants was interrupted by the ascendancy of the Gehrig-DiMaggio Yankees of 1936 to 1939 and the advent of World War II, in which Greenberg served from 1941 to 1944.

American League from 1936 to 1939. Over his career Greenberg led the AL in home runs and RBI four times each, and compiled a .313 batting average. His career .605 slugging percentage is the fifth-highest of all time. Despite retiring early and missing five full seasons to military service and an injury (in 1936), Greenberg amassed 331 career home runs.

On July 26, 1938, Greenberg hit his 30th and 31st homers of the year, and followed with two more the next day. *The New York Times* reported that Greenberg had hit his 33rd home run seven games before Ruth had in 1927. By July 29 Greenberg had 35, and on August 1 he had 37; the country began to take notice. Greenberg had a mediocre August, hitting only 9 home runs, but he remained ahead of Ruth's pace. Asked in early September whether he could break Ruth's record, he responded, "I've heard that question so much...that I even hear it in my sleep." Beyond the stifling pressure that accosts all players chasing a record, Greenberg had to contend with volleys of racial epithets from opposing players and hostile fans. Hank hit number 47 on September 9, number 51 on September 16, and number 54 on September 21, which meant Greenberg was still three games ahead of Ruth's pace. Number 57 was an inside-the-park home run hit on September 26; number 58 reached the bleachers in the same game.

Hank Greenberg did not hit a home run in his last five games, after connecting for 11 in seventeen days. Many fans, Jews and Gentiles alike, believed that the pitchers, motivated by anti-Semitism, refused to give Greenberg anything to hit during those last games. However, Greenberg himself dismissed that theory, calling it "pure baloney." Rather, Greenberg attributed his failure to strong pitching, some missed opportunities (some long fly balls curved just foul), and cavernous Municipal Stadium in Cleveland, where Greenberg played his final game of 1938.

Hack Wilson swings for a portrait late in his career, with the Brooklyn Dodgers. While with the Dodgers from 1932 to 1934, Wilson occasionally displayed the brilliance he had exhibited on a daily basis only a few years earlier with the Chicago Cubs. Hack was a top-flight star for the great Cubs teams of the late 1920s, and his 1930 season ranks among the greatest ever.

HACK WILSON: 56 IN '30

Hack Wilson probably thought he had a lot to atone for after the 1929 World Series. The hard-hitting, hard-drinking star center fielder for the Chicago Cubs lost two fly balls in the sun during the seventh inning of Game Four, which allowed the A's to score ten runs in the frame and come back from an 8-0 deficit to win the game. Instead of the Series being tied 2-2, the A's led 3-1 and closed out the Series on the next day. During the 1930 season the goat of the previous World Series would make amends by partially rewriting the NL record book.

Hack Wilson did not look like a ballplayer. He was only five-foot-six and had a huge upper body planted atop short stubby legs and tiny feet. However, when he put his 210 pounds into a pitch he could give it a ride. He was a great ballplayer—when he was sober, that is. After playing well for the pennant-winning New York Giants in 1924, Wilson behaved so erratically that he was relegated to the minors in 1925. The Cubs purchased him for a mere $5,000 before 1926, and as his play improved he became known as the "million-dollar slugger from the five-and-dime store." From 1926 to 1930 Wilson was one of the National League's most feared sluggers. In retrospect, the key to Wilson's performance was his relationship with his manager. While Joe McCarthy was the Cubs skipper Wilson prospered; McCarthy tolerated Wilson's drinking as long as he played well. But once the strict Rogers Hornsby replaced McCarthy in 1931, Wilson's game fell apart. Wilson descended from the pinnacle of major league glory in 1929 and 1930 to the minors by 1935, and was out of baseball entirely by 1936. In only one season, Wilson's production dropped from 56 home runs, 190 RBI, and a .356 average in 1930 to 13 home runs, 61 RBI, and a .261 percentage in 1931.

Wilson was a certified star slugger before 1930, but he will always be remembered for the one season he posted numbers unrivaled in the annals of the senior circuit. There was more offensive production in the National League in 1930 than in any other major league in baseball history, and no one produced like Hack Wilson. On August 26 he broke Chick Klein's one-year NL record of 44 home runs. At the beginning of September Wilson was ahead of Ruth's 1927 pace, 46 to 43 home runs, but Hack could not match Ruth's great September. Nevertheless, on September 20 he broke Lou Gehrig's all-time record for the most RBI in a season. He crushed two homers on September 27 to reach number 56, with one game left in the season. The next day he failed to homer, but added two RBI for a still-unsurpassed total of 190, one of baseball's greatest milestones.

BABE RUTH: 54 IN '20

The Babe moved down the coast from Boston to Gotham and surpassed his previous home run record of 29 by mid-season in 1920. Before the gloom cast by the Black Sox scandal spread over baseball in September, Ruth fever had swept New York and the entire nation. Fans packed the Polo Grounds every day to witness the mighty Babe Ruth, setting an attendance record that would not be broken until 1946. The Babe led the Yankees into their first pennant race ever with a .376 average and a still-unbroken record .847 slugging percentage. In 1948 Ruth reflected on his 1920 performance: "People found it hard to believe, when I finally hit 54 that year, as fans of today would react to, say, some kid who hit 200." That is a slight—but only slight—exaggeration.

BABE RUTH: 54 IN '28

His highness the Sultan of Swat had another monster year in 1928. The Yankees' offense just wasn't the same as it had been in 1927, but the decline in Ruth's numbers (down to 54 home runs, 142 RBI, and a .323 average from 60 home runs, 158 RBI, and a .356 average) was less severe than the decline of his teammates' numbers. Nevertheless, the pinstripes swept another World Series. In the 1928 Series Ruth batted .625 with 3 home runs (all in the final game).

RALPH KINER: 54 IN '49

Ralph Kiner led the National League in home runs in each of his first seven seasons. No other player, not even Babe Ruth, won seven consecutive home run titles, let alone in his first seven years of major league play. In an era dominated by the home run, Kiner was the game's most prolific slugger. The 1949 season was his greatest.

In the years following World War II Ruth's 1927 home run total was the most sought-after record in all of baseball. So many careers had been truncated by the war that the golden 714 mark seemed beyond reach. Therefore, sluggers concentrated on the task of reaching 60, while the media speculated about who could make the best run at the record. By 1949 a consensus had emerged: Ralph Kiner, the strapping young slugger from the lowly Pittsburgh Pirates, was the man most likely to do it. In fact, Kiner's persona was that of a player in pursuit of 60. While the Bucs floundered in the second division, Kiner's clouts made him a heartthrob to the bobby-soxed girls, a hero to the boys, and a boost to game attendance across the United States.

Kiner's preoccupation with the pursuit of 60 earned him a reputation as a one-dimensional, selfish player. Yet Kiner's numbers were exceptional, as good as anyone's in the National League at the time except for Stan Musial's. Kiner undoubtedly would have made a great contribution to a winning club (though his home run totals would have been lower away from Pittsburgh, where he had a mandate to swing for the fences at all times).

Ralph Kiner joined the Cleveland Indians for his final season in 1955. Kiner retired at the age of thirty-three, having already hit 369 home runs, because of injury. His ratio of 1 home run per 14.11 at-bats is the third highest ever, behind Babe Ruth (11.76) and Mark McGwire (13.21). Had Kiner maintained that ratio and batted as often as Henry Aaron, he would have smashed 877 home runs.

Kiner kept a steady, though not record-breaking, pace over the balance of the 1949 season. Then he had a spectacular September—virtually equaling Ruth's performance in the last month of the 1927 season—in which he hit 16 homers to give him 54 for the year. Kiner finished the season with a league-leading 127 RBI; he was also tops in the league in walks (137) and slugging percentage (.627), and finished fifth in the batting race with a .310 average.

MICKEY MANTLE: 54 IN '61

By September 10, 1961, Mickey Mantle, of M&M fame (with Roger Maris), had 53 home runs when he contracted "this cold, virus, or I don't know....Anyway, I felt awful!" Mantle mentioned his condition to his friend, Mel Allen, the radio announcer. Allen brought the superstar center fielder to his doctor for a shot "that could take care of everything." Mantle recalled, "It knocked me on my butt, was what it did. The doctor hit a bone with a needle. Then my side got infected...[the next day] I went to the hospital....I was dizzy and had a 104-degree temperature. They looked at my side, lanced it and took an X-ray. They said the bone was bruised and I had all sorts of problems." One problem was that his role in the season-long home run derby with Maris was effectively over. Mick came back to play down the stretch, but he only managed to belt one more home run.

The on-deck circle forms a halo around Mickey Mantle as he blasts his 52nd home run of 1961, on September 8. With the balance of a month left, the Mick still had a good shot at hitting 60, but an illness and a protracted recovery soon sidelined him and left Roger Maris to chase Ruth's record by himself. Nonetheless, Mantle was somewhat of an angelic figure during 1961. As a Yankees veteran he was the crowd favorite in the quest to catch Ruth, but he never failed to provide emotional support and guidance to the high-strung Maris.

Having himself suffered the wrath of Yankees fans at the beginning of his career, Mantle remained supportive of Maris, providing guidance for his high-strung teammate. Mantle recalled: "After a while he came to me and said 'I can't take it anymore, Mick.' And I had to tell him. 'You'll have to take it, you'll just have to.'" Following Maris' death in 1985, Mantle commented that "the greatest single feat I ever saw was Roger Maris hitting 61 home runs to break Babe Ruth's record. I was with him practically every step of the way, and I know the dues he paid to get there."

MICKEY MANTLE: 52 IN '56

Mantle exploded in May 1956, belting 16 home runs during the month. On Memorial Day Mantle was at the top of the majors in home runs (20), RBI (50), and batting average (.425). He cooled off later in the season, but he never relinquished his lead in any of the AL triple-crown categories. From mid-May on, the New York press tracked Mantle's progress against Ruth's 1927 home run total. The last of the dynastic Yankees superstars had come of age.

WILLIE MAYS: 52 IN '65

At Shea Stadium on August 29, 1965, Willie Mays broke Ralph Kiner's record for the most home runs in August with his 17th round-tripper of the month. Kiner was working as the Mets announcer at the time and was obliged to interview Willie after the game. However, it was Willie who asked the most poignant question: "Are you sore?" "Of course I'm sore," Kiner replied. "Wouldn't you be?" Willie Mays was still charming the United States with his unique, improvised manner. He was also still knocking the covers off baseballs.

Mays' season had started with a flourish: he had belted ten home runs by May 7. Mays continued to produce, but by the end of July his home run total was merely 24. Then came a very productive August. Mays finished out the season with a strong September as he led the Giants on a heartbreaking quest for the pennant—the Dodgers captured the flag on the last weekend of the season. Nonetheless, Mays won his second NL MVP award (eleven years after he had won his first). Over the season, Mays compiled 52 home runs, 112 RBI, and a .317 average. At the age of thirty-four Mays was at the top of his game.

Willie Mays is congratulated by on-deck batter Willie McCovey as the Say Hey Kid crosses home plate at the Astrodome after hitting his 500th career home run on September 13, 1965. The blast was Mays' 47th of the 1965 campaign and placed him only 11 home runs shy of Mel Ott's all-time NL record of 511. Mays hit his 512th NL home run on May 4, 1966. Henry Aaron, who passed Mays in career homers on June 10, 1972, now holds the career NL record with 733.

GEORGE FOSTER: 52 IN '77

When fans reminisce about the Big Red Machine of the mid-1970s, the names spoken with the most awe are Johnny Bench, Joe Morgan, Tony Perez, and, of course, Pete Rose. With good reason, these four greats all starred for the Reds across the balance of the decade, and they never seemed to have off-years. The player who contributed the most firepower to the Big Red Machine from 1975 on, however, was George Foster (even in the championship years of 1975 and 1976, only Morgan created more offense than Foster).

Foster bounced around the minor leagues and some major league benches for five full seasons before emerging as a star on a world championship team in 1975. He then led the National League in RBI for three straight years (a record), won two consecutive home run titles, and established himself as one of baseball's most feared hitters. He was traded to the Mets in 1982, becoming the highest-paid player in baseball, and flopped. His dog days in New York severely tarnished his reputation. He retired in 1986 with a .274 average (it was .286 before he joined the Mets) and 348 home runs.

In 1977, however, George Foster was nothing short of awesome. Not only did he become the first major league player in twelve years to surpass 50 home runs, hitting 52, but he knocked in 149 runs, batted .320, and set a Reds record with 388 total bases. His home runs were not hit in clusters but spread evenly across the whole season. Foster had 45 home runs by September 4, but failed to make a strong run at the record. He hit number 50 on September 23 with only seven games left in the season. He established a new record for right-handed batters by crushing 31 homers on the road. He was a consensus NL MVP selection.

JOHNNY MIZE AND RALPH KINER: 51 IN '47

Two players have hit 50 or more home runs in the same season twice in AL history, in 1938 and 1961. This phenomenon has only occurred once on the senior circuit, in 1947 by Johnny Mize of the New York Giants and Ralph Kiner of the Pittsburgh Pirates. All summer long Kiner was chasing Mize, and the fans tracked their progress,

While George Foster was a kind and deeply religious man in private, he was an intimidating presence at the plate with his black bat and menacing gaze. For seven full seasons, from 1975 through 1981, Foster terrorized NL pitchers. After signing a multimillion-dollar contract with the Mets in 1982, Foster failed to produce. The Mets remained a last-place team and Foster's previous team, the Reds, fell into the second division in his absence.

Johnny Mize takes a cut at the Polo Grounds on June 2, 1947. The "Big Cat" ranks eighth on the all-time list in career slugging percentage, and his home run total of 359 would have been higher if not for the three years he missed due to service in the U.S. Navy during World War II. From his early years with the Cardinals through his peak with the Giants to the twilight of his career on champion Yankees teams, Mize was a feared slugger.

Ralph Kiner bats for the Pirates during his prime, in which he won or shared an unprecedented seven consecutive NL home run titles (1946 to 1952). Because of his power-hitting exploits, Ralph was unfairly labeled a one-dimensional player. If Kiner had played for a contending team he would have impressed upon the baseball public that he was an exceptional all-around hitter.

wondering if the two sluggers could match the Babe's phenomenal pace of twenty years earlier. As it turned out, Mize and Kiner both finished with 51 home runs.

Johnny "Big Cat" Mize is one of the most overlooked sluggers in major league history. Owner of a lifetime .312 average and 359 career home runs, Mize had a career that spanned from 1936 to 1953. He played for the Cardinals until 1941, and he holds their franchise record for the most home runs in a season (43). He moved to the Giants for the 1942 season, then spent the next three years in the U.S. Navy. He resumed playing for the Giants from 1946 to 1949. In August 1949 he was traded to the Yankees, with whom he stayed until his retirement (contributing to five consecutive World Series titles as a spot-starter and pinch hitter). A strong, six-foot-two, 215-pound, left-handed first baseman, Mize won or shared four NL home run titles, four slugging percentage titles, three RBI crowns, and one batting title (he averaged .349 in 1939). He batted better than .300 his first nine years in the majors. His

slugging percentage in the NL, .577, is second only to Rogers Hornsby's .578.

Mize and Kiner ended the season in a head-to-head race for the NL home run crown, although their respective seasons couldn't have started more differently. Mize crushed 3 consecutive home runs on April 24, which equaled Kiner's total output during the first six weeks of the season. While Mize exploded out of the starting gates, Kiner, the defending NL home run champ, was mired in a sophomore slump. However, Kiner's new teammate and childhood idol, Hank Greenberg, pulled Ralph aside and gave him some advice that got the youngster back on track. Trailing Mize 14 to 3 at the end of May, Kiner broke his own Pirates team record with his 24th and 25th home runs of the season on July 23. Nonetheless, Mize still led the league with 31. On August 16 Kiner hit 3 successive home runs in a game against the Cardinals, and tied the record with 7 home runs in four games. By the end of August, Kiner had 39 home runs to Mize's 43. On September 12 Kiner concluded another home run spree by setting a new record by

hitting 8 homers in four games, and finally surged ahead of Mize. On September 18 Kiner hit number 50, but Mize caught him at that milestone on September 20. Kiner hit 51 on September 23, and Mize hit 51 two days later. Succumbing to the pressure, neither slugger could connect during the final three days of the season.

WILLIE MAYS: 51 IN '55

In 1955 the Say Hey Kid followed his 1954 batting title and MVP award with the season's home run crown. However, 1955 was the season in which Mays finally encountered adversity, as the Giants failed to win the pennant for the first time in his career. It was no fault of his: he finished second in batting with a .319 average, led the league in slugging, compiled 127 RBI, and stole 24 bases in 28 attempts. And, of course, he played incomparable center field. He hit his 49th and 50th homers with six days left in the season, one in each game of a doubleheader, to give him 7 home runs in six consecutive games.

CECIL FIELDER: 51 IN '90

In 1989 Cecil Fielder tore up the league with 38 home runs in only 384 at-bats—the Japanese league, that is. From 1985 to 1988 Fielder was a part-time player for the talent-laden Toronto Blue Jays. Stranded behind the slick-fielding, equally powerful Fred McGriff at first base, and unable to secure a starting role as designated hitter because of George Bell, Fielder decided it was time to move on—all the way to Japan. No player had ever returned from Japan and made a significant impact in the majors, but the Detroit Tigers were

willing to take the risk, having had their poorest season ever in 1989 (they finished with the worst record in baseball, 103 losses). Fielder made a huge impact, and the Tigers improved by more than twenty games.

Cecil's home run production was very steady across the whole season. He was in a spectacular race with Oakland A's superstar Jose Canseco until August, when chronic back problems began to limit Canseco's power. For his part, Fielder kept right on hitting home runs and having an amazing season. By September 3 the six-foot-three, 230-pound Fielder had 43 home runs. With five games

to go Cecil reached 49. At first he thought clubbing number 50 would be no problem, but his teammates noticed that he was pressing. It came down to the final game of the season in Yankee Stadium. With the pennant races all determined, the national media was on hand. Fielder did not disappoint them, blasting 2 home runs and becoming the first player in thirteen years to reach the 50 milestone.

JIMMIE FOXX: 50 IN '38

Foxx's accomplishment in 1938 was largely overshadowed by Hank Greenberg's assault on Ruth's record. Foxx blasted two home runs, numbers 43 and 44, on September 10 to close within 3 of Greenberg, who answered the challenge by belting 3 homers over the next two days. Nonetheless, Foxx had an amazing year, not only setting the Red Sox record for the most home runs in a season, but also leading the league in RBI (175), batting average (.349), and slugging percentage (.704). In almost any other year Foxx would have won the triple crown.

Above: Cecil Fielder joined the Detroit Tigers in 1990 after he spent a year in Japan. He instantly established himself as one of the game's premier sluggers, becoming the first player in thirteen years to top 50 homers in a season and the first AL player to do it in twenty-nine years. Fielder did not let up after 1990; he led the majors in RBIs again in 1991 and 1992, becoming the only player besides Babe Ruth to win three consecutive RBI titles. Right: Jimmie Foxx is seen here at a Red Sox training camp late in his career. For all the hype about Fenway Park being a right-handed power-hitter's paradise, Foxx was the only Red Sox slugger ever to knock 50 homers in a season.

ALBERT BELLE: 50 IN '95

After suffering without a pennant for four decades, the Cleveland Indians front office tried a different tactic in the early nineties: they signed their most talented young players to lucrative long-term contracts. Thus, the Indians were committed to building a winner around a nucleus of center fielder Kenny Lofton, second baseman Carlos Baerga, catcher Sandy Alomar, Jr., and their crown jewel, slugger Albert Belle. In 1994, this group led the Tribe into contention when, to the dismay of pennant-starved Cleveland, the strike-shortened season ended in mid-August. Belle had led the way with a .357 batting average, 101 RBIs, and 36 round-trippers, which put him on pace to hit 50.

The Indians rebounded from the disappointment and played brilliantly from day one in 1995, racing away with their first pennant in forty-one years. Belle was productive but not spectacular: he had only 19 home runs through July. He heated up in August, knocking out 14 dingers, and then he caught fire, tying Babe Ruth's 1927 record for homers in September with 17; Belle's 31 homers in that two-month span is an all-time record. Home run number 50 came in the second-to-last game of the season, making Belle the first player ever to have at least 50 home runs and 50 doubles (he had 52) in the same season. And because the 1995 season was only 144 games long, Belle's numbers were truly extraordinary.

Behind the mighty bat of Albert Belle, the 1995 Indians sailed into the postseason with the best record in Major League Baseball.

The Saga of Jose Canseco

Sluggers have occasionally reached the middle of the season on pace to hit 60, and even 70, home runs, yet failed to reach even 50. One dramatic example was the Oakland A's Jose Canseco in 1990.

Canseco won the AL Rookie of the Year award in 1986. He fully blossomed in 1988, when he became the only player in major league history to hit 40 home runs and steal 40 bases; he won the AL MVP that year and led the A's to their first of three consecutive AL pennants. Jose was slowed by a wrist injury in 1989, but he returned to the team by mid-season and played well as the A's went on to win the World Championship. Then came 1990.

At mid-season Canseco was in a thrilling race with Cecil Fielder of the Detroit Tigers for the lead in home runs in the American League. After falling behind Fielder because of a debilitating back injury, Canseco returned to the lineup in July and caught fire. By August 2 Canseco had surpassed Fielder 34 to 33 in home runs, though Jose had missed twenty-one games! Batting .307 with 82 RBI, Jose was the focus of the national sports media, which proclaimed that the moody A's slugger was playing ball at the level of a Ruth or Mays. Per at-bat, Canseco was well ahead of Maris' pace in 1961, and even with the missed games he was on pace for 60. His mere presence seemed to dominate games. However, Canseco's back trouble resurfaced and the Oakland slugger hit only 1 more homer in August. He failed to regain his form in September, and finished the season with a mere 37 homers, 101 RBI, and a .274 average. Then his sluggish outfield play turned Canseco into the goat of the 1990 World Series.

Despite occasional flashes of brilliance over the next three seasons, Canseco failed to regain his mid-1990 form. Then in 1994, with the Texas Rangers, Canseco again became one of baseball's most feared sluggers. In the strike-shortened season, he blasted 31 home runs, batted .282 with 90 RBI, and even stole 15 bases. Jose played for Boston in 1995, and after spending much of the first half of the season on the disabled list, he came back hitting .306 with 24 home runs and 81 RBI—helping the Red Sox to the Eastern Division title.

A young Jose Canseco takes a swing for the Oakland A's.

Baseball's Most Famous Home Runs

Frank Baker is captured here batting for the Philadelphia A's a few years before his legendary nickname was coined during the 1911 World Series. "Home Run" Baker was a large man and an agile hitter; if he had played in a later era he probably would have hit many home runs. In his day, however, 2 dramatic World Series blasts were enough to earn him a moniker that guaranteed him a place in the history of power-hitting.

Fate and circumstances determine who comes to bat at the decisive moment of a baseball game. Consequently, many of baseball's greatest moments involve otherwise obscure players. The game's most celebrated round-trippers include not only the record-breaking blasts of legendary sluggers, but also home runs by less accomplished men who were in the batter's box at the right time and rose to the occasion to gain immortality.

HOW "HOME RUN" BAKER GOT HIS NAME

The 1911 World Series matched the defending champion Philadelphia A's against the New York Giants, a team that featured legendary manager John McGraw and pitching aces Christy Mathewson and Rube Marquad. The A's were led

by their "$100,000" infield of first baseman Stuffy McInnis, second baseman Eddie Collins, shortstop Jack Barry, and third baseman Frank Baker. The Giants won Game One, 2-1, thanks to Mathewson's pitching. In Game Two the score was tied 1-1 when Marquad surrendered a double to Collins with two out in the sixth inning. Baker was up next. Though first base was open and the dangerous Baker had a .334 average, 115 RBI, and a league-leading 9 home runs that year, it made sense for the southpaw Marquad to try to retire the left-handed Baker. Marquad challenged Baker, and the A's cleanup hitter smashed a home run over the right-field fence. The A's won 3-1.

Following Game Two Mathewson's daily newspaper column criticized Marquad for pitching carelessly to Baker. Mathewson got the start in Game Three, and shut down the A's through eight innings; the Giants led 1-0. In the ninth inning, with one out, Baker stepped up to the plate. Mathewson delivered and Baker crushed another home run to right field, tying the score. The A's went on to win the game 3-2. The next day, Marquad's newspaper column questioned whether Mathewson had been too "careless" against Baker. The A's won the Series in six games, and their third baseman was known forever after as "Home Run" Baker.

BABE RUTH'S 60TH HOME RUN

With two games left in the 1927 season Babe Ruth had already tied his record of 59 home runs in one season. He had also hit a homer in each of his last three games. On the next to last game of the sea-

son, pitcher Tom Zachary decided enough was enough; he wasn't going to give the streaking Bambino anything to hit. In the first inning Zachary walked the Babe on four straight pitches. Later on, with the score tied and runners on first and third, the Babe stepped up again. Still intent on not giving Ruth any material to work with, Zachary tossed a curve ball at the slugger, hoping to hit him. However, the Babe didn't even step back; instead he began his swing and met the pitch in front of his right hip and pulled it around the right-field foul pole for his 60th home run. It was his 25th homer in 41 games—there was just no stopping the Bambino toward the end of 1927.

BABE RUTH'S "CALLED SHOT"

Babe Ruth's most celebrated home run occurred during the third game of the 1932 World Series. The Philadelphia A's had beaten the Yankees for the AL pennant from 1929 to 1931; therefore 1932 represented the Sultan of Swat's first Series appearance in four years. The NL opponents were the Chicago Cubs. Considerable ill will existed between the Cubs and Yankees. Yankees manager Joe McCarthy was seeking revenge for being fired after the Cubs lost the 1929 World Series; at the time Cubs owner William Wrigley had said he

wanted a manager "who can get me a world championship." Furthermore, Yankees players were outspoken over the mistreatment of former Yankee Mark Koenig, who had played brilliantly for the Cubs after a trade but was allotted only a half share of World Series pay. The Cubs, in turn, resented the Yankees for meddling in their business.

The Yankees won the first two games handily in New York. On October 1, 1932, Game Three began with Ruth hitting a three-run homer with nobody out in the first inning. The Cubs clawed back, and entering the fifth inning the score was tied 4-4. With one out Ruth stepped up to the plate—what followed is the stuff of legend and controversy. The Cubs' cries of "Big Belly" and "Balloon-head" greeted the aging slugger. Ruth responded to the jeering with a grin, and before stepping in to face pitcher Charlie Root, he waved his bat towards the outfield. The first pitch was a called strike. Ruth calmly looked over at the Cubs' bench and said, "That's one." More jeering from the dugout. After two balls, Root threw another called strike. The crowd and the Cubs roared. Ruth stepped out of the box, held up two fingers, and said, "That's two." He then turned to Cubs catcher Gabby Hartnett and said, "It only takes one to hit it." Before stepping in Ruth pointed his bat toward center field again. Root delivered a curve ball and Ruth drove the ball over the center field wall.

Newspaper accounts of the game challenge this legendary account of the "called shot." It is well established that Ruth counted out the strikes in response to the Cubs' name-calling. However, most onlookers claim that any gesture made by Ruth with his bat was part of an exchange with the pitcher. Regardless, Ruth had succeeded in homering dramatically while openly taunting the Cubs. Ruth would never confirm nor deny accounts of the legendary event. Years later he described the scene after the homer: "How the mob howled. Me? I just laughed and laughed to myself going around the bases, thinking about what a lucky bum I was." Lou Gehrig followed Ruth with another home run and the Yankees won the game 7-5, and eventually swept the Series.

Lou Gehrig greets Babe Ruth at home plate after the Bambino hit a grand slam, his 59th home run in 1927. Dutch Ruether, Earle Combs, and Mark Koenig scored in front of the Babe. Ruth blasted 16 grand slams during his career, but it is Gehrig who holds the all-time record with 23. Willie McCovey is second with 18 and Eddie Murray tops active players with 17.

GABBY HARTNETT'S "HOMER IN THE GLOAMING"

In mid-season 1938 the Chicago Cubs were in third place—six and a half games behind the first-place Pirates—when the Cubs ownership named their veteran star catcher Gabby Hartnett the new player-manager. The Cubs responded to the leadership of the good-natured Irishman, and by September they were playing consistently well and closing in on the Pirates. Winning seven straight games, the Cubs closed to within one and a half games of Pittsburgh with a week left in the season. And the Pirates were coming to Chicago for a decisive three-game series.

The Cubs won the first game behind the pitching of the legendary Dizzy Dean. The next day, September 28, 1938, the game was tied 5-5 at the end of the eighth inning. Daylight was waning and the park had no lights; the umpires convened and decided to play one more inning. If the game was still tied after the ninth then a doubleheader would be played the next day—a severe disadvantage for the Cubs, whose pitchers' arms were exhausted. The Pirates were retired in short order in the top of the ninth. Likewise, Pittsburgh reliever Mace Brown quickly got two outs. Up to the plate stepped thirty-seven-year-old manager Gabby Hartnett. Brown threw two fast balls, both strikes. Then Hartnett swung at a curve and rocketed the ball into the left-field bleachers. Chicago

won 6-5. As night fell over the Windy City, the Cubs held first place. The Cubs won again the next day 10-1 to sweep the series, then coasted to the pennant over the demoralized Pirates.

BOBBY THOMSON'S "SHOT HEARD 'ROUND THE WORLD"

In 1951 the New York Giants made two of the greatest comebacks in baseball history: the first was spread across fifty days; the second lasted one third of an inning. The first comeback made heroes out of Giants manager Leo Durocher and rookie Willie Mays, and the second transformed infielder Bobby Thomson into a living legend.

On August 11 the Giants were virtually eliminated from pennant contention, thirteen and a half games behind the first-place Brooklyn Dodgers. The Giants won their next three games, and then swept the Dodgers three straight. Ten games later the Giants had won sixteen straight and were only five games back. In the final week of the season the Giants trailed by two and a half games, but won their last four games while the Dodgers lost four of seven, resulting in a tie. The Giants had won thirty-seven of forty-four games since August 11, forcing a three-game playoff for the NL pennant.

The Giants and Dodgers split the first two games, which led to an all-or-nothing game at the Polo Grounds on October 3. The game was tied 1-1 at the beginning of the eighth inning when the Dodgers combined four singles and a walk to score three runs against fatigued Giants hurler Sal Maglie. The Giants failed to score in the eighth and came to bat in the ninth facing a three-run deficit. Alvin Dark led off the inning with a scratch single off tiring Dodger ace Don Newcombe. Don Muellar followed with a single to right field that moved Dark to third. Monte Irvin fouled out, but Whitey Lockman sliced a double to left that scored Dark with Muellar stopping at third. Dodger Manager Chuck Dressen walked to the mound and called for Ralph Branca, proud wearer of uniform number 13, to replace Newcombe. The first batter Branca faced was the power-hitting Bobby Thomson, who had hit a two-run homer off Branca during game one of the playoff. The first pitch of their rematch was a called strike. The second was a belt-high fastball that Thomson turned on and sent deep to left field. Giants announcer Ross

Gabby Hartnett prepares for the 1938 season, during which he became player-manager of the Cubs and hit a dramatic home run to lead his team to the pennant. One of the greatest catchers of all time, Hartnett blasted 236 homers and batted .297 over a twenty-year career.

Bobby Thomson is still in the batter's box and the ball is still in the air, but this touched-up photograph traces the path the ball eventually traveled on its way to the left-field stands in the Polo Grounds. Thomson's home run was so wildly celebrated by Giants fans that such photos remained hanging on people's walls in New York City for years.

Hodges' famous radio call captured the emotion of the moment when Thomson's shot landed in the left-field stands: "The Giants win the pennant! The Giants win the pennant! The Giants win the pennant! Bobby Thomson hits it into the lower deck of the left-field stands. The Giants win the pennant! And they're going crazy! They're going crazy! I don't believe it! I don't believe it! The Giants win by a score of 5 to 4. And they're picking Bobby Thomson up and carrying him off the field...."

BILL MAZEROSKI'S NINTH-INNING BLAST

Bill Mazeroski, one of the greatest defensive second basemen of all time, was immortalized with one swing of the bat on October 13, 1960. A Pittsburgh Pirate for seventeen seasons, this West Virginia native was signed out of an Ohio high school in 1954 and debuted in the majors in 1956.

Fans mob Pittsburgh's Bill Mazeroski as he rounds third base following his Series-winning blast. It's every child's dream to come to bat in the ninth inning of the seventh game of the World Series with the score tied and hit a home run. Appropriately, when Mazeroski did just that, every Pirates fan was delirious.

A defensive wizard, Maz teamed with veteran shortstop Dick Grant as the defensive foundation around which the Pirates built their 1960 championship team. Maz won eight Gold Gloves and set records for most double plays in a career and in a season. Maz was a consistently productive batter, but not a feared slugger. Ironically, he hit one heroic longball that secured his place in baseball lore, overshadowing a superlative defensive career.

The 1960 World Series was rife with offense. The upstart Pirates, who had not been to the Fall Classic in thirty-three years, split the first six games with the dynastic Yankees in an unorthodox fashion. The Pirates outscored the Yankees 14-8 in their three victories, while the Yankees had walloped the Pirates 38-3 in the other three games. Game Seven began with the Pirates grabbing an early 4-0 lead, only to have the Yankees fight back and seize control of the game 7-4 by the eighth inning. In the bottom of the eighth the lead-off hitter for the Pirates singled. Then Bill Virdon hit what should have been a routine double-play grounder—instead, the ball took an impossible bounce and smashed Yankees shortstop Tony Kubek in the throat, temporarily debilitating him. From there the Pirates struck for five runs, taking a 9-7 lead after eight innings. The Yankees battled back to tie the game in the top of the ninth.

Bill Mazeroski led off the bottom of the ninth. On Ralph Terry's second pitch of the inning, Mazeroski sent a shot over the left-field wall. Pandemonium erupted at Forbes Field—the Pirates had won 10-9 and were World Champions. Maz's blast was the first home run ever to end a World Series, and remains the only homer to break a tie in either half of the ninth inning of a World Series seventh game.

ROGER MARIS' 61ST HOME RUN

Roger Maris entered the final game of the 1961 regular season with 60 home runs and the weight of the world on his shoulders. Regardless of the asterisk (and all that it symbolized), to surpass 60 homers in a season would be to enter uncharted territory, where Roger Maris would stand alone. October 1, 1961, offered a once-in-a-lifetime opportunity and a last chance to silence the critics. After flying out to left in the first inning, Maris

stood in against Boston's Tracy Stallard with one out in the fourth inning of a scoreless game. After two balls Stallard delivered a fair pitch, which Maris—his huge biceps bulging under his short sleeves—sent soaring into the right-field stands for his 61st home run. Appropriately, the game ended 1-0.

HENRY AARON'S 715TH HOME RUN

Babe Ruth's record of 714 home runs, perhaps the most cherished statistical record in all of baseball, no longer seemed invulnerable at the end of the 1973 season. Henry Aaron of the Atlanta Braves had finished the season with 713 career home runs. Aaron had gained on Ruth's record because of unprecedented home run production past the age of thirty-five, including 40 homers in 1973, when Aaron was thirty-nine years old. Barring a freak injury, Aaron was poised to shatter the record in 1974.

In the season opener in Cincinnatti, Aaron homered on his first swing to tie Ruth's record. Atlanta management vowed that Aaron would set the mark at home. Aaron played sparingly the next few games, and returned to Atlanta, for a nationally televised home opener on April 8. In a circus atmosphere, amid death threats tinged with ugly racial slurs, Aaron walked in the second inning without swinging once. The next time Aaron came up to bat was in the fourth inning against Al Downing, the Dodgers' left-handed starter. The first pitch was a change-up that bounced in front of the plate. The next pitch was a fastball, and on his first swing of the night—arguably his first true swing since opening day and only his second of the season—Aaron belted the ball over the left-center-field wall for his 2nd home run of the season and the 715th of his career.

Roger Maris connects for his record-breaking 61st home run of 1961, securing a place among baseball's immortals. Maris' grimace betrays not only his intensity as a hitter but also the pressure he endured as he closed in on Babe Ruth's hallowed record. Maris' swing conveys power and grace, and shows that no amount of pressure could interefere with his performance as a slugger.

The whole world was watching on April 8, 1974, when Henry Aaron hit his 715th career home run, breaking Babe Ruth's record. In the United States, a nationwide television audience watched. The next morning Henry's feat was headline news across the globe. However, one man who did not see the ball clear the left-center-field fence was Aaron himself. After he had hit the ball, he put his head down and ran hard toward first base, as he usually did. It wasn't until he saw first base coach Jim Busby jumping up and down that Aaron knew he held baseball's most cherished record.

Carlton Fisk's Eleventh-Hour Homer

In 1993 Carlton Fisk was released in mid-season by the Chicago White Sox, having caught more games than any catcher in major league history—a tremendous achievement, by any standards. Nevertheless, the power-hitting New England native will be remembered mostly for his performance in the wee hours of October 22, 1975.

Rain delayed Game Six of the 1975 World Series, which the Reds were leading over the Red Sox 3-2, for three days. So far the Series had been exceptionally well played and exciting, but Game Six would exceed all expectations. Early on, the Red Sox led 3-0, thanks to rookie sensation Fred Lynn's three-run homer. The Reds scored three in the fifth, when Lynn crashed into the outfield wall

chasing a triple by Ken Griffey. The Reds then added two runs in the seventh, and an insurance run in the eighth on a home run by Cesar Geronimo. Leading 6-3, the Big Red Machine sensed a championship. Then, with two on and two out in the bottom of the eighth, pinch hitter Bernie Carbo crushed a home run to center. The game remained tied 6-6 for two innings, though not for lack of drama: in the ninth, the Red Sox had a runner thrown out at the plate; in the eleventh, Dwight Evans robbed the Reds' Joe Morgan of a two-run homer at the right-field wall.

Carlton Fisk led off at the bottom of the eleventh. Pitcher Pat Darcy delivered his first pitch to Fisk, and the Red Sox catcher blasted the ball into the New England night sky, down the left-field line, curving.... Standing to the right of the batter's box, Fisk watched his shot and pleaded with the

Above: Carlton Fisk sends a ball soaring into the evening, down the left-field line, and over the Green Monster. Fisk's twelfth-inning home run ended what many have called one of the greatest games ever played: Game Six of the 1975 World Series, between the Red Sox and the Reds. Right: Fisk's teammates prepare to mob the slugger as he approaches home plate.

ball to stay fair, jumping up and down, waving his arms, and using every gesture of body English conceivable. The ball hit the foul-pole netting, making it a fair ball. Fisk's home run ended what many consider the greatest, most dramatic game ever.

CHRIS CHAMBLISS' ALCS HOMER

The once (or rather three-time) dynastic Yankees had not won a pennant in twelve years when Billy Martin led a hungry mix of homegrown talent and imported veterans to the AL East title in 1976. Characteristic of the team was Chris Chambliss, a consistent, clutch-hitting first baseman whose professionalism masked his unwavering desire to win. In the ALCS, the pinstripes met a young exciting team from Kansas City that filled the void left in the AL West by the dismantling of the A's dynasty of the early 1970s. The Royals and the Yankees split the first four games dramatically, leaving one game to decide the pennant.

The Yankees took an early lead and held it until the eighth inning, when George Brett's three-run home run tied the game 6-6. In the top of the ninth, the Yankees narrowly averted disaster when the Royals had two runners on and a ground ball up the middle produced a controversial forced out. Chambliss led off at the bottom of the ninth.

Above: Chris Chambliss gets mobbed by fans as he rounds the bases following his pennant-winning home run. Above right: Chambliss connects, sending a rocket into the stands and the Yankees back to the World Series for the first time in twelve years. Chambliss' blast led off the bottom of the ninth in the fifth and decisive game of the 1976 ALCS between the Yankees and the Royals.

Right-handed flamethrower Mark Littel challenged the left-handed Chambliss, who turned on a fastball and sent it into the right-field bleachers. With one swing Chambliss brought the pennant back to the Bronx.

HOW REGGIE JACKSON BECAME "MR. OCTOBER"

"I'm the straw that stirs the drink," declared a defiant Reggie Jackson midway through the turbulent 1977 season (his first as a Yankee). Jackson no doubt meant to imply that his presence—what he brought to a team—would catapult the Yankees beyond the previous year's accomplishment (an AL pennant) to their first World Series title in fifteen years. What Jackson's comment ultimately betrayed about Reggie was that he, like Muhammad Ali, welcomed the added pressure, the hype, and the media glare. When the Yankees had captured the AL East and then the pennant in dramatic fashion, the stage was set for Reggie to carry the team to the championship or to choke on his words.

After a slow start in the first two games, split in New York, Jackson went 5 for 11 with 2 home runs (one in his last at-bat) as the Yankees won two of three in Los Angeles. In Game Six, Reggie took over. After walking on four pitches and scoring in the second inning, Reggie came up in the fourth with a runner on first base, no outs, and the Dodgers leading 3-2. He promptly fired Burt Hooton's first pitch over the right-field wall. In the next inning, Reggie batted with one runner on, two out, and the Yankees up 5-3. Once again he sent the first pitch into the right-field stands. When Reggie led off the bottom of the eighth, with the score unchanged, Yankee Stadium rocked to chants of "Reggie, Reggie!" Knuckleballer Charlie Hough delivered his first pitch, and Jackson blasted it into the center-field bleachers for his third home run on three pitches (his fourth on four consecutive swings, dating back to Game Five in Los Angeles) to tie Babe Ruth's single-game World Series record and establish a new record of five home runs in one Series. Jackson had clinched the championship in spectacular fashion, which he had all but promised, and gained the title of "Mr. October."

According to many Red Sox fans it was the "curse of the Bambino" that provided the diminutive Bucky Dent with the power to lift a Mike Torrez pitch over the Green Monster and lead the Yankees to victory over the Red Sox in the one-game playoff that decided the epic 1978 AL East race. Legend has it that the Red Sox have been cursed since they traded Babe Ruth to the Yankees in 1920.

BUCKY DENT'S "SHOT HEARD 'ROUND NEW ENGLAND"

Ironically, the final hero of the dramatic 1978 AL East pennant race, which was highlighted by the exploits of legends like Reggie Jackson, Jim Rice, Ron Guidry, and Carl Yastrzemski, was the Yankees' diminutive shortstop Bucky Dent. The defending champion Yankees were in disarray at mid-season, fourteen and a half games behind the Red Sox on July 9. The Yankees replaced fiery manager Billy Martin with soft-spoken Bob Lemon on July 25. The team responded to the change and went on a tear, quickly gaining on the Red Sox. By September 7 the Yankees had moved within four games of first place as they began a four-game series in Boston. The Yankees not only swept the series, but humiliated the Red Sox, outscoring them 46 to 9. However, after the Yankees had built a three-and-a-half-game lead, the Red Sox rebounded, winning twelve of their last fourteen games (including their last eight), to catch the Yankees and finish in a tie for first. A one-game playoff, to be played on October 2—a Monday afternoon—in Boston, would determine the champion of the division.

Yastrzemski opened up the scoring for the Sox with a solo homer off Guidry in the second inning. Rice added an RBI in the sixth. Red Sox pitcher Mike Torrez had cruised through the first six innings, but in the seventh Chris Chambliss and Roy White led off with singles. Normally the Yankees would have used a pinch hitter for Bucky Dent in this situation, but with regular second baseman Willie Randolph injured, the Yankees had already exhausted their supply of infielders. Torrez started Dent off with a slider low and inside, which Dent hit off his ankle. Limping around, Dent thought Torrez might try the same pitch again. Indeed, Torrez followed with another slider, and Dent golfed it toward left field. Behind the plate Carlton Fisk first thought the hit was a pop-up: "then I saw [left-fielder] Yaz looking up and I said 'Oh God.'" As Dent rounded the bases, Fenway Park was dead silent except for the clapping of the Yankees players and management: the home run had put the Yankees in the lead 3-2.

The Yankees added another run in the seventh, and then Reggie Jackson hit a titanic homer in the eighth. The Red Sox mounted a comeback in their half of the eighth, scoring two runs off relief ace Goose Gossage. With the score still 5-4 in the bottom of the ninth, Gossage retired the first but walked the second hitter. The next man up lifted a routine fly ball to right field, which Lou Pinella lost in the lights. Pinella bluffed like he was going to catch the ball, which froze the base runner; miraculously the ball bounced right in front of Pinella who picked it up and held the lead runner at second. Then Jim Rice flew out to Pinella, the

Reggie Jackson crushes his record-breaking 5th home run of the 1977 World Series (opposite, top) and pauses to appreciate the flight of the ball (opposite, bottom). Jackson once said, "The only reason I don't like playing in the World Series is I can't watch myself play."

The Most Famous All-Star Game Home Run

·······························.

The American League trailed 5-3 heading into the bottom of the ninth inning of the 1941 All-Star Game at Briggs Stadium in Detroit. Up to that point Arky Vaughn, the flashy Pittsburgh shortstop, had been the hero of the game—he had connected for 2 home runs. In the final frame, the AL loaded the bases with one out on two singles and a walk. Cubs right-hander Charlie Passeau then faced Joe DiMaggio. The Yankee Clipper grounded a perfect double-play ball, but second baseman Billy Hermann pivoted and threw wide to first base, allowing one run to score. The score was 5-4 with men on first and third, two out, and Ted Williams at bat. Passeau got ahead of Williams with one ball and two strikes. But then Williams crushed Passeau's fourth pitch beyond right field and against the facade above the third tier of the stadium. The American League won 7-5—with one swing of his mighty bat Williams shone brighter than any star.

Above: Joe DiMaggio and Coach Marv Shea congratulate Ted Williams as he crosses home plate after his winning blast in the All-Star Game in 1941. Williams had a batting average of .406 in 1941, the last time a major leaguer hit over .400, and DiMaggio hit in a record fifty-six consecutive games during that summer. Right: Ted Williams relaxes against a batting cage.

runner advancing to third. With everything on the line, Gossage enticed Yastrzemski to pop up to third base for the final out.

In one of the most dramatic games ever, little Bucky Dent hit the home run that turned the game around, upstaging a cast of legends to become the hero of the day.

GEORGE BRETT AND THE PINE-TAR INCIDENT

Universally revered as a great line-drive hitter, George Brett of the Royals displayed his power with some of the most dramatic home runs of his time: a three-run shot to tie the decisive game of the 1976 ALCS; three homers in one ALCS game against the Yankees in 1978 (the Royals lost the game and the series); another three-run homer off Goose Gossage to lift the Royals over their nemesis, the Yankees, in the 1980 ALCS; and three home runs, all off Doyle Alexander, to lead the Royals past Toronto in the 1985 ALCS. Nevertheless, Brett's most famous home run (albeit dramatic in its conventional context) is renowned for the controversy that ensued after the pitch, the swing, the flight of the ball, and the circling of the bases.

The setting on July 24, 1983, is classic Brett: Yankee Stadium, Royals trailing 4-3, top of the ninth, one man on, two out, Gossage on the mound. Gossage delivers one of his patented, terrifying fastballs; Brett crushes the ball into the right-field stands, putting the Royals up 5-4. Not so fast—Yankees manager Billy Martin pops out of the dugout, approaches the home-plate umpire, and registers a protest. The umpires convene and request to see Brett's bat. The umpires study the bat, measure it against home plate, and talk some more, and then home-plate umpire Tim McClelland signals Brett out. The game is over; the Yankees win 4-3. Brett comes storming out of the dugout like a man possessed, face boiling over with rage, looking ready to tear McClelland's head off. Restrained by his teammates and the other umpires, Brett is finally dragged back to the clubhouse. The Yankees hit the showers, apparent victors.

The Royals file a formal protest over the umpire's decision to declare Brett out for using pine tar on the surface of his bat beyond the

seventeen inches from the handle allowed in the major leagues because Billy Martin had brought it to the attention of the umpires following Brett's home run. Two days later, AL President Lee MacPhail upheld the Royals' protest (overruling an umpiring crew for the first time in league history), noting that Martin, who admitted learning of the excess pine tar on Brett's bat two weeks prior to the game, should have lodged his protest long before the game was played. Thus, MacPhail credited the Royals their two runs and set a date, August 18, on which the game would be resumed—two outs, top of the ninth, Royals ahead 5-4.

The game ended 5-4.

Left: George Brett heads towards first, having lashed one of his signature line drives. Brett was one the purest hitters of all time. Playing in Kansas City's cavernous Royals stadium, Brett slapped balls to all corners of the outfield. However, on the road in the post-season (especially at Yankee Stadium with its short right field), Brett was a power-hitting terror. Above: The umpires have just declared Brett out for hitting a homer, or so George sees it. Umpire Joe Brinkman restrains an enraged Brett, while umpire Tim McClelland holds the famed pine-tarred bat. Kansas City manager Dick Hauser is trying to make sense of it all and keep Brett out of prison.

Kirk Gibson's World Series Triumph

Kirk Gibson always had a flair for the dramatic; never was it more evident than during Game One of the 1988 World Series. In 1984 the fleet-footed, power-hitting outfielder had dominated the post-season spotlight on a well-balanced Detroit team that led the AL East from start to finish. In 1986 Gibson had set a major league record with five consecutive game-winning RBI. In 1988 the often-injured star skipped out on his native Michigan for the bright lights of Los Angeles, where his infectious enthusiasm coupled with the virtually unhittable pitching of Orel Hershiser led the Dodgers to a surprise pennant.

Gibby starred in the NLCS, but his aching legs left him on the "doubtful" list for the World Series, to be played against the young, heavily favored Oakland A's. In Game One, Gibson sat idly on the bench as the A's carried a 4-3 lead into the ninth inning. Ace reliever extraordinaire Dennis Eckersley retired the first two batters. Then pinch hitter Mike Davis reached base. Dodgers manager Tommy Lasorda called on

Kirk Gibson celebrates while rounding the bases following his game-winning, bottom-of-the-ninth, pinch-hit home run off ace reliever Dennis Eckersley in the first game of the 1988 World Series. The scenario surrounding Gibson's homer was so dramatic—the wounded star had limped off the bench in a last-ditch effort to foil the heavily favored A's—that one announcer remarked that such a series of events could only happen in Hollywood.

Joe Carter heads towards first base and a place in baseball lore, having just crushed a World Series–winning home run in Game Six of the 1993 Fall Classic. Carter was the team leader and cleanup hitter for the back-to-back champion Toronto Blue Jays (1992 and 1993). Carter was always a star slugger; he contributed 100-RBI seasons for the Indians, the Padres, and the Blue Jays. Yet it took his World Series home run swing to make him a celebrity.

Gibson, bypassed once already, to bat. Gibson limped to the plate, and soon after fell in the hole with zero balls and two strikes. In fact, on the first four pitches all Gibson could muster up was four weak foul balls. The fifth pitch was a slider, which Gibson lunged for and connected with, sending the ball rocketing into the right-field bleachers. Pandemonium ensued on Chavez Ravine. Gibson, perhaps himself in disbelief, rounded the bases pumping his arms and practically dragging his wounded legs. Gibson did not appear again in the Series, which the Dodgers won 4-1; indeed, the Dodgers never let the A's get close after Gibson's improbable blast.

JOE CARTER'S WORLD SERIES WINNER

No World Series had ever ended on a come-from-behind multi-run homer until 1993, when Joe Carter, Toronto's reliable RBI man and inspirational leader, blasted his way into baseball lore (the only Series that had ever ended on a home run was in 1960, when Bill Mazeroski broke a tie with a round-tripper).

The defending champion Toronto Blue Jays were leading the Series 3-2, but had already failed to close out the Phillies in Game Five. The Phillies furthered their momentum by overcoming a four-run deficit in Game Six. Going into the bottom of the ninth, the Phillies held a 6-4 lead. However, the lead was far from secure as the Blue Jays were sending their powerful top-of-the-order against the Phillies' beleaguered closing pitcher Mitch "Wild Thing" Williams. True to form, Williams walked Ricky Henderson to start the inning, and then surrendered a sharp single to center by Devon White. Williams seemed to gain control and composure and retired the always difficult Roberto Alomar. Next up was the clean up hitter Joe Carter, who watched a few of Williams' pitches sail outside, fouling off a couple of pitches along the way. With the count at two balls and two strikes, Williams came in with a slider that Carter crushed high and deep to left field. Would it be fair or foul? It landed over the wall, fair as they come. In that instant the Blue Jays became the first team to repeat as World Champions in fifteen years, and Joe Carter became a baseball legend.

The Most Famous Pinch-Hit Home Run

The most celebrated pinch-hit home run in baseball history ended the first game of the 1954 World Series, the same game in which Willie Mays made his miraculous running catch to rob Vic Wertz. Thanks to Mays' catch in the eighth, the game headed into extra innings with the Indians and the Giants tied 2-2. The Indians failed to score in the top of the tenth inning. After one out in the bottom of the tenth, Mays walked and then stole second. The Indians then walked Henry Thomson to bring up Monte Irvin, who was susceptible to the double play. However, Giants manager Leo Durocher countered with the left-handed pinch-hitting sensation Dusty Rhodes to face Cleveland ace Bob Lemon. On Lemon's first pitch Rhodes sent a towering fly ball down the right-field line that barely cleared the wall just under 300 feet from home plate. Indians fans griped about the "pop-up home run," but it didn't matter to New Yorkers—Rhodes was the toast of the town. Cleveland never recovered from Mays' and Rhodes' magic; the Giants swept the highly favored Tribe in the Series 4-0.

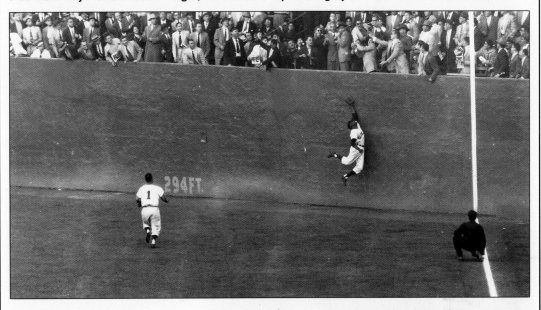

Above: Dusty Rhodes' game-winning, pinch-hit home run just clears the right-field fence at the Polo Grounds, less than 300 feet away from home plate, as Indians right fielder Dave Pope leaps high against the wall in Game One of the 1954 World Series. Rhodes followed his "pop-up home run" by blasting a 350-foot homer in Game Two of the Series. Right: Dusty Rhodes approaches home plate as his teammates prepare to mob him in celebration of Rhodes' home run, the winning blast in Game One of the 1954 World Series for the Giants. Because of Rhodes' great 1954 season, he is remembered by many as one of the greatest pinch hitters of all time. Rhodes was truly remarkable in 1954, batting .333 as a pinch hitter in the regular season (15 for 45) and collecting important pinch-hit RBIs in the first three games of the World Series (including home runs in Game One and Game Two). However, Rhodes was never much of a pinch hitter either before or after 1954; in fact his average as a pinch hitter (excluding the 1954 season) was well below .200. It only goes to show that any player can become a legend if he's in the right place at the right time.

The 1990s and Beyond

In the 1980s and early 1990s the trend in major league baseball was toward less offense, especially fewer home runs (with the notable exception of 1987, when a record 2.12 homers per game were hit). In 1993 this trend reversed dramatically, and in 1994 home runs were being hit in record numbers—until a labor dispute ended the season prematurely. The 1995 season saw a dropoff from the '94 boom, but still qualified as a great offensive year.

The game of baseball is constantly evolving; in the 1970s offensive strategy moved away from power hitting toward speed; during the 1980s, the two most notable changes in the game involved pitching. The most distinctive change was the increased importance of relief specialists, especially the advent of setup men and one-inning closers. A team behind after seven innings can now expect to face two expert pitchers accustomed to performing well in tense situations. Also, the presence of late-inning specialists takes pressure off the starters, who know they only have to pitch well for six or seven innings (instead of nine) to get a win. Consequently, batters rarely face tired pitchers. The other recent pitching innovation is the development of the split-fingered fastball, a breaking ball thrown at full velocity. Since the split-fingered pitch drops down, very few batters can hit home runs off the pitch.

In this era of increased pitching expertise, offensive strategy involves the use of any weapon available to a team: power hitting, speed, sacrificing, and the hit-and-run. Teams with large stadiums tend to emphasize speed, while tenants of small stadiums still try to stockpile sluggers. The

Ken Griffey, Jr., of the Seattle Mariners is the closest thing to Willie Mays since the Say Hey Kid himself. Son of Ken Griffey, star outfielder for the great (Cincinnati) Big Red Machine of the 1970s, Junior can do it all: he's a spectacular center fielder; he hits for average; and he grabs headlines with his spectacular home run barrages. In mid-1993 he tied Dale Long and Don Mattingly's record by hitting home runs in 8 consecutive games, and in his first playoff appearance Griffey Jr. tied Reggie Jackson's mark for the most home runs in a postseason series, with 5 against the Yankees in the 1995 divisional playoffs.

Eddie Murray, pictured in his prime with the Baltimore Orioles, now plays for the revitalized Cleveland Indians. If Murray, a model of consistency throughout his career, reaches the 500 milestone, he will be the first player to do so without hitting 40 home runs in any season.

Through 1995 Dave Winfield had hit 465 home runs and driven in 1,833 runs over twenty-three major league seasons. If Winfield plays in 1996, his twelfth RBI will move him past Carl Yastrzemski and into tenth place on the all-time list.

Andre Dawson was one of three active players with more than 400 home runs in 1995. A top-flight star for more than a decade with the Expos and Cubs, Dawson has become a productive part-time player, and veteran leader, for the Florida Marlins.

tremendous amount of player movement from team to team, due to free agency, has further facilitated the emergence of a new breed of player who combines speed and power. Among this group are some of the game's brightest stars: Barry Bonds, Ken Griffey, Jr., and Roberto Alomar. The entire St. Louis Cardinals outfield of Bernard Gilkey, Brian Jordan, and Ray Lankford, though not as accomplished, also fits this mold.

A number of contemporary players are compiling impressive career slugging statistics. Among the older generation of active players, three men have already eclipsed the 400 home run plateau: Andre Dawson, Dave Winfield, and Eddie Murray. Dawson had hit 436 home runs through the 1995 season, and will likely play only one more year. Winfield had compiled 465 career homers but had hit only 12 the previous two seasons, and at age forty-four, it seems unlikely that he will reach 500. Murray, however, has a legitimate chance to join the 500 Club. A central component of the powerful Cleveland attack, Murray batted .323, drove in 82 runs, and belted 21 homers to help the Indians to the 1995 AL pennant. In the process, Murray surpassed Winfield as the home run leader among active players and

The irrepressible Barry Bonds has already won three NL MVP awards—two with Pittsburgh and one with San Francisco. He may become the first four-time MVP in major league history.

finished the season with a career total of 479. At forty years of age, Murray could have a few more productive years and may be able to eclipse Mickey Mantle's record for home runs by a switch-hitter (536).

Among the sluggers now in their prime, four outstanding figures—Darryl Strawberry, Jose Canseco, Mark McGwire, and Kevin Mitchell—are truly representative of their generation because their careers have been hampered by injuries or other off-field impediments. Strawberry had 280 home runs when he was twenty-nine, yet he will begin the 1996 season with only 297 at age thirty-four. Canseco's total of 300 round-trippers at age thirty-one would have been much higher if not for back and arm injuries. Thirty-two-year-old McGwire has compiled 277 homers, and he missed more than half the A's games the past three seasons. In fact, less spectacular but ever-steady Fred McGriff, virtually the same age as McGwire, surpassed Mark two seasons ago and now has 289 career home runs. Oft-injured Kevin Mitchell, who has blasted 220 major league homers, reestablished himself as a top-flight slugger two seasons ago at age thirty-three, but then chose to play in Japan in 1995—which reminds fans of thirty-two-year-old Cecil Fielder, who has avoided injury but has only 250 home runs because of the years he spent on the Blue Jay bench or in Japan.

Though born in the same month and year as Jose Canseco, Barry Bonds is marketed as the marquee star (alongside Ken Griffey, Jr.) of baseball's new generation. Not a power hitter during his early years with the Pittsburgh Pirates, Bonds emerged as a top-flight slugger in the nineties. Barry tied for the major league lead in home runs with 46 in 1993, when he won his third NL MVP Award in four years. In 1994, he overcame a nagging elbow injury to blast 37 round-trippers and managed to pound out 33 more in '95 (an "off-year" for Bonds) to raise his career total to 292.

An era of low offense in baseball came to an abrupt end in 1993. Run production increased from 8.23 runs per game in 1992 to 9.20 in 1993, and the number of home runs rose dramatically from 1.44 per game in '92 to 1.77 in '93.

Throughout the 1993 season the increase in offense was attributed to the expansion of the National League, which added franchises in Florida and Colorado. History has shown that expansion thins the pitching talent without adversely affecting batters' statistics: the year that Roger Maris hit 61 homers, 1961, was an expansion season in the American League. Thus, most experts believed that pitching would rebound in 1994 from the drubbing it had taken in 1993.

Contrary to people's expectations, however, the 1994 season was an unprecedented slugfest and all-around offensive explosion. To the delight of fans and batters, baseballs were flying out of major league stadiums. Matt Williams, Frank Thomas, Ken Griffey, Jr., and newcomer Jeff Bagwell (who was born on the same day of the same year as Thomas) became household names as they embarked on an assault of Roger Maris' single-season home run record and other sundry

offensive records. Tony Gwynn was batting .391 two-thirds of the way through the season and was poised to challenge the hallowed .400 mark, which was last transcended by the Splendid Splinter, Ted Williams, in 1941.

The overall statistics for the 1994 season are stunning. Runs per game rose to 9.54, one of the highest in major league history. The overall batting average in the American League was .273, the highest since 1921; in the National League it was .267, the highest since 1930. The average number of home runs hit per game was 2.06 — the second highest in major league history.

During the 1994 season, fans, players, and journalists offered their theories on the increase in offense. The two most popular hypotheses were that the baseball itself was too lively (i.e., it had been "juiced") and that the recent expansion had severely thinned the pitching talent. Indeed, the top-ranked pitchers were immune to the

No one lost more to the labor dispute that killed the end of the 1994 season than San Francisco Giants third baseman Matt Williams: through 115 games, Williams led the majors with 43 home runs, which put him on pace to hit 61 homers over the course of a 162-game season. Williams was even more brilliant at the beginning of the 1995 season: through 35 games he was leading in home runs (13), RBI (35), and batting average (.381) when he broke a bone in his foot, sidelining him for two months.

Chicago's Frank Thomas has produced Ted Williams–type numbers since he became the White Sox's starting first baseman during the 1990 season. Many baseball analysts believe that combined slugging percentage and on-base percentage approximate the overall worth of a batter. Through 1995, the "Big Hurt," who won the AL MVP in 1993 and 1994, has a career .593 slugging percentage and a .455 on-base percentage for a combined 1.048, which would rank him fourth all-time (if he had enough career at bats to qualify for the all-time list), after only Babe Ruth (1.163), Williams (1.116), and Lou Gehrig (1.080).

offensive explosion. Aces David Cone, Jimmy Key, Mike Mussina, Ken Hill, Brett Saberhagen, and (especially) Greg Maddux had excellent seasons. However, in general, hitting talent far exceeded pitching talent during the 1994 season; juiced ball or not, this was the primary reason for the offensive explosion. While Greg Maddux and David Cone might have been able to retire the likes of Jeff Bagwell, Kevin Mitchell, Albert Belle, or Frank Thomas, few other pitchers could. While a whole generation of hitting superstars seemed to come of age in 1994, there seemed to be a dearth of young pitching talent.

The offensive statistics of the stars of 1994 are awe-inspiring. At the head of the class was the Astros' Jeff Bagwell. An up-and-coming star in 1993, Bagwell exploded in 1994, hitting .367 with 39 home runs (on pace for 55) and 116 RBI (on pace for 163). His on-base percentage was .451 and his slugging percentage was .750, the second highest in NL history (to Rogers Hornsby's .756 in 1925) and seventh-best overall. In the American League, both the White Sox's Frank Thomas and the Indians' Albert Belle had almost comparable numbers.

However, it was San Francisco Giant Matt Williams who led the majors in homers with 43, while Ken Griffey, Jr., appropriately led the junior circuit with 40. Williams, Griffey, Bagwell, Thomas (38), Barry Bonds (37), and Belle (36) were all on pace to hit 50 homers—a feat that had been done only once in each league over the past twenty-eight seasons. Matt Williams' home run total is especially miraculous: having hit 43 round-trippers in 115 games, Williams was on pace to hit exactly 61 homers for the season.

Fans across North America were exhilarated by the 1994 major league home run derby. At the end of every month, excitement filled the air as Williams, Griffey Jr., and Thomas set new standards for homers hit in the months of May, June, and July...and then came August 12. From that fateful day onward, nothing but silence emanated from the cathedrals of America's national pastime in 1994. A labor dispute closed down the most

Cleveland Indian Albert Belle was one of six young sluggers—along with Matt Williams, Ken Griffey, Jr., Jeff Bagwell, Frank Thomas, and Barry Bonds—who were on pace to hit 50 home runs during the strike-aborted 1994 season. However, Belle made up for the lost opportunity when he managed to slam 50 home runs in the strike-shortened 1995 season of 144 games, becoming only the twelfth player in major league history to reach that milestone.

thrilling season in memory, and for the first time in ninety years there was no World Series.

By spring training there was still no settlement. The clubs fielded teams (with the exception of Baltimore) made up of sub–minor league "replacement players" in order to start the season on time; a very ugly scene was growing uglier. Fortunately, a court ruling in late March forced the owners to accept the conditions of the previous collective bargaining agreement until a new agreement could be reached, and the players ended their strike. However, the season would have to start late, and each team would only be able to play 144 games. Thus, none of the 1994 sluggers could realistically hope to set a new single-season home run record.

The 1995 season started dismally. Fans, furious at owners and players alike for betraying them the previous year, stayed away from the game. But as the season wore on, the fans slowly returned. On the field, the 1995 season was once again rife with offense. Home run hitting was still near a record level, at 2.02 per game; the number of runs scored actually increased from 9.54 in 1994 to 9.70. The Colorado Rockies' power surge made headlines; playing in the thin mountain air, the Rockies

became only the second team in history besides the 1977 Dodgers to have four players (Dante Bichette, Larry Walker, Vinny Castilla, and Andres Galarraga) collect 30 home runs in a season. While no player made a run at Maris' record because of the shorter season, Albert Belle went on an astounding home run tear at the end of the season, blasting a record-setting 31 home runs in the last two months of the season to finish with 50. The 1995 postseason was thrilling, and at year's end, it seemed that the scars created by the labor debacle were beginning to heal.

Seventy-five years ago, the game's greatest slugger, Babe Ruth, mesmerized the nation with his power and led baseball through the dark days of its previous great crisis—the Black Sox scandal. Today, a new generation of sluggers are in an analogous position, ready to propel baseball back into the hearts of the millions of fans who suffered during the strike and its aftermath. Indeed, rarely have so many promising young sluggers appeared in the majors at the same time. Matt Williams has 225 homers at age thirty; Albert Belle is only twenty-nine and already has 194; and 1995 World Series hero Dave Justice is roughly the same age as Belle and has 154.

A trimuvirate of stars who finished the 1995 season at twenty-seven years of age hover around 100 career homers: Jeff Bagwell (113), Boston's Mo Vaughn (111), and the Dodgers' Mike Piazza (92). However, Frank Thomas, Ken Griffey, Jr., and Texas Ranger Juan Gonzalez are off to an even more prodigious start. Thomas has 183 home runs at the age of twenty-seven, while Griffey Jr. has 189 at twenty-six. Gonzalez, who is roughly the same age as Griffey, won the AL home run titles in 1992 and 1993 and has already crushed 167 balls over major league fences. All three are on pace to make the list of all-time leaders, earn a place at Cooperstown, and enter the realm of legend. Perhaps all three of these young sluggers will avoid injury and climb their way into the 500 Club, and perhaps one will surpass 600 career homers and join ranks with the likes of Mays, Ruth, and Aaron. And just maybe, one will hit career home run 756.

A P P E N D I X

Career Statistical Line for the Top 16 Home Run Kings.

		HR	G	AB	H	2B	3B	R	RBI	BB	K	SB	SA	BA
1.	Hank Aaron	755	3298	12,364	3771	624	98	2174	2297	1402	1383	240	.555	.305
2.	Babe Ruth	714	2503	8399	2873	506	136	2174	2204	2056	1330	123	.690	.342
3.	Willie Mays	660	2992	10,881	3283	523	140	2062	1903	1463	1526	338	.557	.302
4.	Frank Robinson	586	2808	10,006	2943	528	72	1829	1812	1420	1532	204	.537	.294
5.	Harmon Killebrew	573	2435	8147	2086	290	24	1283	1584	1559	1699	19	.509	.256
6.	Reggie Jackson	563	2820	9864	2584	463	49	1551	1702	1375	2597	228	.490	.262
7.	Mike Schmidt	548	2404	8352	2234	408	59	1506	1595	1507	1883	174	.527	.267
8.	Mickey Mantle	536	2401	8102	2415	344	72	1677	1509	1734	1710	153	.557	.298
9.	Jimmie Foxx	534	2317	8134	2646	458	125	1751	1921	1452	1311	88	.609	.325
10.	Ted Williams	521	2292	7706	2654	525	71	1798	1839	2019	709	24	.634	.344
	Willie McCovey	521	2588	8197	2211	353	46	1229	1555	1345	1550	26	.515	.270
12.	Ernie Banks	512	2528	9421	2583	407	90	1305	1636	763	1236	50	.500	.274
	Eddie Mathews	512	2388	8537	2315	354	72	1509	1453	1444	1487	68	.509	.271
14.	Mel Ott	511	2734	9456	2876	488	72	1859	1861	1708	896	89	.533	.304
15.	Lou Gehrig	493	2164	8001	2721	535	162	1888	1990	1508	789	102	.632	.340
16.	Eddie Murray	479	2819	10,603	3071	532	34	1545	1820	1257	1403	105	.482	.290

Best Home Run Ratio (minimum 1,000 games).

		HR	AB	Ratio
1.	Babe Ruth	714	8399	11.76
2.	Mark McGwire	277	3659	13.21
3.	Ralph Kiner	369	5205	14.11
4.	Harmon Killebrew	573	8147	14.22
5.	Ted Williams	521	7706	14.79
6.	Dave Kingman	442	6677	15.11
7.	Mickey Mantle	536	8102	15.12
8.	Jimmie Foxx	534	8134	15.23
9.	Mike Schmidt	548	8352	15.24
10.	Fred McGriff	289	4512	15.61
11.	Hank Greenberg	331	5193	15.69
12.	Jose Canseco	300	4711	15.70
13.	Willie McCovey	521	8197	15.73
14.	Lou Gehrig	493	8001	16.23
15.	Darryl Strawberry	297	4843	16.31
16.	Henry Aaron	755	12,364	16.38
17.	Willie Mays	60	10,881	16.49
18.	Hank Sauer	288	4796	16.65
19.	Eddie Matthews	512	8537	16.67
20.	Willie Stargell	475	7927	16.69
21.	Rob Deer	226	2831	16.95
22.	Frank Howard	382	6488	16.98
23.	Kevin Mitchell	220	3742	17.01
24.	Frank Robinson	586	10,006	17.16
25.	Barry Bonds	292	5020	17.19
26.	Steve Balboni	181	3120	17.21
27.	Bob Horner	218	3777	17.33
28.	Roy Campanella	242	4205	17.38
29.	Rocky Colavito	374	6503	17.39
30.	Gus Zernial	237	4131	17.43

Most Home Runs by Position, Career.

1B: 1. Lou Gehrig 493 — ML & AL record
2. Jimmie Foxx 473
3. Willie McCovey 439 — NL record

2B: 1. Joe Morgan 266 — ML record
2. Rogers Hornsby 263 — NL record
3. Lou Whitaker 244 — AL record

3B: 1. Mike Schmidt 509 — ML & NL record
2. Eddie Mathews 482
3. Graig Nettles 319 — AL record

SS: 1. Cal Ripken, Jr. 314 — ML & AL record
2. Ernie Banks 293 — NL record
3. Vern Stephens 213

OF: 1. Babe Ruth 686 — ML & AL record
2. Henry Aaron 661 — NL record
3. Willie Mays 643

C: 1. Carlton Fisk 351 — ML & AL record
2. Johnny Bench 326 — NL record
3. Yogi Berra 313

P: 1. Wes Ferrell 36 — ML & AL record
2. Warren Spahn 35 — NL record
3. Red Ruffing 35

Most Home Runs by Position, Season.

AL:

Hank Greenberg	DET	1938	1B	58
Joe Gordon	CLE	1948	2B	32
Al Rosen	CLE	1953	3B	43
Rico Petrocelli	BOS	1969	SS	40
Roger Maris	NY	1961	OF	61
Carlton Fisk	CHI	1985	C	33
Wes Ferrell	CLE	1931	P	9

NL:

Johnny Mize	NY	1947	1B	51
Rogers Hornsby	STL	1922	2B	42
Davey Johnson	ATL	1973	2B	42
Mike Schmidt	PHI	1980	3B	48
Ernie Banks	CHI	1958	SS	47
Hack Wilson	CHI	1930	OF	56
Roy Campanella	BKN	1953	C	40
Don Newcombe	BKN	1955	P	7
Don Drysdale	LA	1958	P	7
	LA	1965	P	7

Club Career Home Run Leaders.

AL:

Baltimore Orioles	Eddie Murray	333
St. Louis Browns	Ken Williams	185
Boston Red Sox	Ted Williams	521
California Angels	Brian Downing	222
Chicago White Sox	Carlton Fisk	210
Cleveland Indians	Earl Averill	226
Detroit Tigers	Al Kaline	399
Kansas City Royals	George Brett	291
Milwaukee Brewers	Robin Yount	235
Seattle Pilots (1969)	Don Mincher	25
Minnesota Twins	Harmon Killebrew	475
Washington Senators (1901–1960)	Roy Sievers	180
Washington-Minnesota Franchise	Harmon Killebrew	559
New York Yankees	Babe Ruth	659
Oakland A's	Mark McGwire	277
Philadelphia A's	Jimmie Foxx	302
Kansas City A's	Norm Siebern	78
A's Franchise	Jimmie Foxx	302
Seattle Mariners	Ken Griffey, Jr.	189
Texas Rangers	Juan Gonzalez	167
Washington Senators (1961–1971)	Frank Howard	237
Washington-Texas Franchise	Frank Howard	246
Toronto Blue Jays	George Bell	202

NL:

Atlanta Braves	Dale Murphy	371
Milwaukee Braves	Eddie Mathews	452
Boston Braves	Wally Berger	199
Braves Franchise	Henry Aaron	733
Chicago Cubs	Ernie Banks	512
Cincinnati Reds	Johnny Bench	389
Houston Astros	Jimmy Wynn	223
Los Angeles Dodgers	Ron Cey	228
Brooklyn Dodgers	Duke Snider	316
Dodgers Franchise	Duke Snider	389
Montreal Expos	Andre Dawson	225
New York Mets	Darryl Strawberry	252
Philadelphia Phillies	Mike Schmidt	548
Pittsburgh Pirates	Willie Stargell	475
St. Louis Cardinals	Stan Musial	475
San Diego Padres	Nate Colbert	163
San Francisco Giants	Willie McCovey	469
New York Giants	Mel Ott	511
Giants Franchise	Willie Mays	646
Colorado Rockies	Dante Bichette	88
Florida Marlins	Jeff Conine	55

Club Single-Season Home Run Leaders.

AL:

Baltimore Orioles	Frank Robinson	49	1966
St. Louis Browns	Ken Williams	39	1922
Boston Red Sox	Jimmie Foxx	50	1938
California Angels	Reggie Jackson	39	1982
Chicago White Sox	Frank Thomas	40	1995
Cleveland Indians	Albert Belle	50	1995
Detroit Tigers	Hank Greenberg	58	1938
Kansas City Royals	Steve Balboni	36	1985
Milwaukee Brewers	Gormon Thomas	45	1979
Seattle Pilots	Don Mincher	25	1969
Minnesota Twins	Harmon Killebrew	49	1964,1969
Washington Senators (1901–1960)	Roy Sievers	42	1957
	Harmon Killebrew	42	1959
New York Yankees	Roger Maris	61	1961
Oakland A's	Mark McGwire	49	1987
Philadelphia A's	Jimmie Foxx	58	1932
Kansas City A's	Bob Cerv	38	1958
Seattle Mariners	Ken Griffey, Jr.	45	1993
Texas Rangers	Juan Gonzalez	46	1993
Washington Senators (1961–1971)	Frank Howard	48	1969
Toronto Blue Jays	George Bell	47	1987

NL:

Atlanta Braves	Hank Aaron	47	1971
Milwaukee Braves	Eddie Mathews	47	1953
Boston Braves	Wally Berger	38	1930
Chicago Cubs	Hack Wilson	56	1930
Cicinnati Reds	George Foster	52	1977
Houston Astros	Jeff Bagwell	39	1994
Los Angeles Dodgers	Mike Piazza	35	1993
Brooklyn Dodgers	Duke Snider	43	1956
Montreal Expos	Andre Dawson	32	1983
New York Mets	Darryl Strawberry	39	1987,1988
Philadelphia Phillies	Mike Schmidt	48	1980
Pittsburgh Pirates	Ralph Kiner	54	1949
St. Louis Cardinals	Johnny Mize	43	1940
San Diego Padres	Nate Colbert	38	1970,1972
San Francisco Giants	Willie Mays	52	1965
New York Giants	Johnny Mize	51	1947
	Willie Mays	51	1955
Colorado Rockies	Dante Bichette	40	1995
Florida Marlins	Gary Sheffield	27	1994

Most Home Runs in Each Month, Both Leagues.

April:
NL—11   Willie Stargell, Pittsburgh, 1971
          Mike Schmidt, Philadelphia, 1976
AL—11   Graig Nettles, New York, 1974

May:
NL—15   Cy Williams, Philadelphia, 1923
AL—16   Mickey Mantle, New York, 1956

June:
NL—15   Pedro Guerrero, Los Angeles, 1985
AL—15   Babe Ruth, New York, 1930
          Bob Johnson, Philadelphia, 1934
          Roger Maris, New York, 1961

July:
NL—15   Joe Adcock, Milwaukee, 1956
AL—15   Joe DiMaggio, New York, 1937
          Hank Greenberg, Detroit, 1938

August:
NL—17   Willie Mays, San Francisco, 1965
AL—18   Rudy York, Detroit, 1937

September:
NL—16   Ralph Kiner, Pittsburgh, 1949
AL—17   Babe Ruth, New York, 1927
          Albert Belle, Cleveland, 1995

October:
NL—4   Ned Williamson, Chicago, 1884
         Mike Schmidt, Phiadelphia, 1980
         Dave Parker, Cincinnati, 1985
AL—4   Gus Zernial, Chicago, 1950
         George Brett, Kansas City, 1985
         Ron Kittle, Chicago, 1985
         Wally Joyner, California, 1987

Most Consecutive Games with a Home Run, Both Leagues.

NL:	8	Dale Long, Pittsburgh	(8 HRs)	May 19–28, 1956
AL:	8	Don Mattingly, New York	(10 HRs)	July 8–18, 1987
		Ken Griffey, Jr., Seattle	(8HRs)	July 20–28, 1993

Most Career Pinch-Hit Home Runs.

1. Cliff Johnson	20	4. George Crowe	14
2. Jerry Lynch	18	5. Jose Morales	12
3. Smokey Burgess	16	Bob Cerv	12
Gates Brown	16	Joe Adcock	12
Willie McCovey	16	Graig Nettles	12

Most Home Runs by Two Teammates, Lifetime.

1. Hank Aaron 442, Eddie Mathews 421	863	Mil-Atl	1954–1966
2. Babe Ruth 511, Lou Gehrig 348	859	NY Yankees	1923–1934
3. Willie Mays 430, Willie McCovey 384	814	SF Giants	1959–1972
4. Duke Snider 398, Gil Hodges 361	759	Dodg./Mets	1947–1961/1963
5. Jim Rice 382, Dwight Evans 355	737	Red Sox	1974–1989

Most Home Runs by Two Teammates, Season.

1. Roger Maris 61, Mickey Mantle 54	115	Yankees	1961
2. Babe Ruth 60, Lou Gehrig 47	107	Yankees	1927
3. Hack Wilson 56, Gabby Hartnett 37	93	Cubs	1930
Jimmie Foxx 58, Al Simmons 35	93	A's	1932
4. Babe Ruth 46, Lou Gehrig 46	92	Yankees	1931

Most Home Runs by a Team in a Single Season.

1.	240, NY Yankees	1961 (ML & AL record)
2.	225, Minnesota	1963
	225, Detroit	1987
3.	221, NY Giants	1947 (tied for NL record)
	221, Cincinnati	1956 (tied for NL record)
	221, Minnesota	1964

Most Career Grand Slams.

1. Lou Gehrig	23		Babe Ruth	16
2. Willie McCovey	18		Dave Kingman	16
3. Eddie Murray	17	5.	Gil Hodges	14
Jimmie Foxx	17	6.	Joe DiMaggio	13
Ted Williams	17		Ralph Kiner	13
4. Hank Aaron	16		George Foster	13

Top Career Slugging Percentages.

1.	Babe Ruth	.690
2.	Ted Williams	.634
3.	Lou Gehrig	.632
4.	Jimmie Foxx	.609
5.	Hank Greenberg	.605
6.	Joe DiMaggio	.579
7.	Rogers Hornsby	.577
8.	Johnny Mize	.562
9.	Stan Musial	.559
10.	Willie Mays	.557
	Mickey Mantle	.557
11.	Hank Aaron	.555

Only Team in ML History with Three Players with 40 or More HRs.

Atlanta Braves in 1973:
Dave Johnson, 43
Darrell Evans, 41
Hank Aaron, 40

Only Two Teams in ML History with Four Players with 30 or More HRs.

L. A. Dodgers in 1977:	Colorado Rockies in 1995:
Steve Garvey, 33	Dante Bichette, 40
Reggie Smith, 32	Larry Walker, 36
Ron Cey, 30	Vinny Castilla, 32
Dusty Baker, 30	Andres Galarraga, 31

Most Postseason Home Runs.

1.	Mickey Mantle	18*	
2.	Reggie Jackson	16	(10 WS, 6 ALCS)
3.	Babe Ruth	15*	
4.	Yogi Berra	12*	
5.	Duke Snider	11*	
6.	Lou Gehrig	10*	
	Frank Robinson	10	(8 WS, 2 ALCS)
	Lenny Dykstra	10	(6 WS, 4 NLCS)
	Johnny Bench	10	(5 WS, 5 NLCS)
	George Brett	10	(1 WS, 9 ALCS)

* prior to 1969 there was no championship series

Most Home Runs Allowed by a Pitcher, Season.

50, Bert Blyleven Twins 1986
46, Bert Blyleven Twins 1987
46, Robin Roberts Phillies 1956

Most Home Runs Allowed by a Pitcher, Career.

ML:	Robin Roberts, 505
NL:	Warren Spahn, 434
AL:	Frank Tanana, 398

Average Number of Home Runs Hit Per ML Game.

1905	0.27	1920	0.51	1931	0.87	1959	1.83	1968	1.23	1978	1.40	1989	1.46
1910	0.29	1921	0.76	1935	1.08	1960	1.72	1969	1.61	1980	1.43	1990	1.58
1913	0.38	1922	0.86	1940	1.27	1961	1.92	1970	1.76	1983	1.57	1991	1.61
1915	0.31	1923	0.80	1944	0.84	1962	1.86	1971	1.46	1985	1.71	1992	1.44
1916	0.31	1927	0.75	1947	1.27	1963	1.66	1973	1.60	1986	1.81	1993	1.78
1917	0.27	1929	1.10	1950	1.67	1965	1.67	1975	1.39	1987	2.12	1994	2.06
1919	0.40	1930	1.27	1955	1.81	1967	1.42	1977	1.73	1988	1.51	1995	2.02

Bibliography

Aaron, Henry, with Lonnie Wheeler. *I Had a Hammer*. New York: HarperCollins, 1991.

Charlton, James, ed. *The Baseball Chronology*. New York: Macmillan, 1991.

Einstein, Charles. *Willie's Time*. New York: J.B. Lippincott Company, 1979.

Einstein, Charles, ed. *The Fireside Book of Baseball*, Vols. 1–4. New York: Fireside, 1956, 1958, 1968, 1987.

Greenberg, Hank, with Ira Berkow. *Hank Greenberg: The Story of My Life*. New York: Times Books, 1989.

James, Bill. *The Bill James Historical Baseball Abstract*. New York: Villard Books, 1986.

Kubek, Tony and Terry Pluto. *Sixty-One*. New York: Fireside, 1987.

Reichler, Joseph L., ed. *The Baseball Encyclopedia*. New York: Macmillan, 1994.

Ruth, Babe, with Bob Considine. *The Babe Ruth Story*. New York: Signet, 1992.

Sullivan, George. *Home Run*. New York: Dodd Mead and Company, 1977.

Voigt, David Quentin. *American Baseball*, Vols. 1–3. University Park, Pa.: Pennsylvania State University Press, 1983.

Index